INSTEAD

INSTEAD

Norma Shainin

ABOVE YOUR STATION PRESS
SEATTLE
2013

*For Peter, who makes all things possible, and
Christopher, Patrick and Jennifer, who inspire me with their
creativity*

With special thanks to Christopher, my most exacting reader

NIECE

1

I am sitting halfway up the stairs with my feet dangling through the rungs of the banister, observing the adults. Rudy, the cleverest of my uncles, is lighting aunt Hedwig's cigarette across the expanse of Chinese carpet, with a studiousness bordering on adoration. In his practiced, steadfast way, he is becoming drunk. It will be awhile before his fixed gaze and fumbling attentions become a nuisance to her and a few hours yet before his condition is evident to everyone, especially to Lottie, his wife, who will make their excuses, push his arms into the camelhair coat, and dance him to the front door.

Rudy makes a dazzling but failed attempt to catch the ashes as they fall. Already the wet glass has left a ring on my mother's coffee table. He waves in my direction, less a wave than a fluttering of two fingers, releasing more ashes, the gesture one of conspiracy; as a member of his, favored side of the family I, too, am immune to these petty housekeeping concerns.

Hedwig has taken off her shoes. Her feet are resting uncomfortably close to Rudy's. Her chin reposes on her ample bosom. Potato salad for twenty or more people, her contribution to the midnight supper, has been safely delivered into the kitchen. Soon she will fall asleep. But not before Rudy. They are waiting each other out, anticipating the New Year's din and an arousal into hopefulness.

Rudy has slipped off my father's leather moccasins and pulled the knot out of his bow tie, which still hangs about his neck. He is saying something in a voice so low that Hedwig is forced to raise herself from among the sofa cushions to hear.

He offers another cigarette from the silver case; these, along with the scotch being consumed this evening, are smuggled items, booty from Lottie's brief stints as a ship's cook. In my uncle's hands, cigarettes are implements of seduction. I have never known Hedwig to smoke and am astonished to see her accept another.

My father puffs fat cigars. Their smoke creeps into the closets and drawers, clinging to our clothes, to my wool school coat. When it comes in contact with cold air, the coat emits an odor not unlike that given off by the incineration plant. Like something that has burrowed into the earth and died there. My father stubs his cigars out in the bases of flower pots that decorate the house; he believes in the nutritional value of the ashes.

Rudy continues muttering to himself. I think he much prefers his own company, being far more educated than the rest of the family. Among the few details I know of his past is that he had been trained as a chemist and practiced in Augsburg before coming to this country. Lottie has said that Augsburg had none of the modern enticements of nearby Munich and, sooner or later, he would have left regardless of the Depression.

I think that living in Augsburg could not have been much different than living on this particular street in Queens, in this attached brick house. Although my mother and father do not speak, act or dress like the parents of my school friends, our household is almost identical to the others on this block and I feel doomed by this fact.

Lottie and Rudy live, not in a house, but in a rent-controlled apartment in the foreign borough of Brooklyn where the room in which they sleep is painted lilac; a stuffed alligator scrambles up the wall over their bed. My mother says her sister is disposed to certain South American countries because of their similarity to Europe, but I do not see the proof of this in her gifts to us, trays inlaid with the blue wings of Brazilian moths and cowboy clothes from the Argentinian pampas: calf-skin gloves, suede berets and boots buckled across the instep. Lottie and Rudy would never dare to move, their rent is so reasonable, "no matter how much garbage piles up on the side-walk out front."

"It's not completely theirs, not the way this house is ours." My mother feels sorry that Lottie has no garden in which to raise vegetables and flowers, "not even a windowbox."

Now Rudy, the chemist, washes windows. He confided to me that, at one time, he had aspired to become a translator. This confession was just one more confirmation that there is more to my uncle than a pleasing exterior.

We were on the porch staring at the moon, sitting in the straight wooden chairs which are my family's idea of "lounge" furniture. Rudy had taught me the first stanza of the "Marseillaise," infuriating my father who disdains anything French, and paused in the middle of a card trick.

"Translation is a measure of what can be accomplished but is not," he said, expertly shuffling in an effort to confuse me. He seemed to be lecturing to himself.

"Window washing is a much safer occupation; the thought of translating frightens me now." This from a man who clings to the outsides of buildings, although he assures me there are belts and pulleys and scaffolding.

"One would never be finished," he went on. "One would always be looking backwards." He laughed. "Better than looking down, I suppose," but quickly became serious again. "A profession with very little gratification," he said, and sighed.

When I wondered if there was anything satisfying about washing windows, he told me he finished off each with his hand, "the best chamois," like a craftsman signing his work. It was clear from the tone in his voice, this was a subject he preferred not to pursue. At the time, I thought it was the moon's influence that made him so talkative. Against his better judgement, Rudy had let himself become nostalgic. He began to whisper, "You have to be too literal, following in someone else's footsteps. There's no room for one's own spirit," and here he let the cigarette fly. I believed then that I had divined the reason for his drinking, a response to a failed youthful ambition. I admired the stoicism, the gentlemanly, noncomplaining attitude. The graceful surrender to fate. Only for an instant, did I think he might be lazy.

Of course, there is nothing to be done for it, nothing or noone to blame except perhaps The Great Depression. Anything can set my father off harking back to that trying time: a request from Charlotte for a bicycle with thin tires, or my desire to see the latest movie. The lectures are long and impassioned. We children have so much more than he ever dreamed for himself. We are spoiled. He speaks of missed opportunities and necessary compromise. The most sacred of obligations is to feed one's family. To accomplish this, a man does what he must. My mother, who is a charitable person, shakes her head disapprovingly when anything harsh is said about any of the uncles.

"After all, he's a good provider," she counters, a quality that cancels out a multitude of sins.

There are no teachers, doctors, lawyers among the uncles.

No poets, a profession that smacks too much of idleness. While their aptitudes might have led them into loftier fields, it is with their hands that they now work. Perhaps that is where the drinking comes in. It is acceptable, as long as the men don't give themselves over to it with too much enthusiasm. To be passionate about anything, even liquor, is suspicious in this family.

The uncles started their careers here as dishwashers, cooks and house painters, requiring little skill, or at least not using the skills they had brought with them. My father's chosen profession was that of stonemason like his father before him, but the only evidence of this is the wall that runs around our garden and two pillars which hold up the front gate announcing that a family of substance lives inside. With diligence, and not much luck, busboys became head waiters, apprentices became carpenters. One uncle started out on the packaging line in a gum factory and ended up in the office, filling out orders for Chiclets. He takes his lunch to work in a paper bag. My father carries a satchel, the kind professors favor.

It's not his only conceit. He calls himself a decorator; the wooden stair balusters are splattered with different shades of paint to fool the eye into thinking they are made of marble. This is, however, only slightly more successful than the time he attempted to stipple the dining room walls; when he touched his brush to the gold leaves, they curled up and evaporated.

The discrepancy between intellect, schooling and vocation is the greatest in Rudy's case. I don't hold it against him; I reason that if my uncle had remained a chemist, he might never have come to America, might never have met Lottie. Might never have become the focus of my romantic fantasies.

I take care never to ask Rudy a direct question about his past; it would make him think I'm ashamed of his choices. Besides, I don't want to dispel any mystery.

Rudy must have had many women; my aunt would have had nothing to do with him otherwise. He had been married before. No one in our family can lay claim to such notoriety, although my mother's brother, Hans, had a wife who disappeared, taking his two children when she left. It was years before the secret of Rudy's first marriage became known; Lottie met the woman briefly. When she asks Rudy now about that time in his life, he's even less coherent than when he's drinking; it's as if he's forgotten it ever happened. My mother says Lottie should be grateful for this loss of memory; she's certain the entire story will never come out. She, herself, is incapable of telling lies, but is not, however, in awe of the truth. Omissions are acceptable.

All we know of Rudy's family is that he has a sister living in Manhattan. This sister has a child and, for that reason, Lottie and Rudy brave the cold reception they receive whenever they go there. This other niece makes me jealous in a way my own sister does not.

We are better acquainted with Rudy's friends. I'm an accomplice in the tricks these visitors play on my cousins. Sometimes they go too far, confusing the smaller ones, like Frieda, who can't figure out the secret of the Black Magic game; each time it's played, the rules are changed.

These friends write books about animals and live in the Catskills or Blue Ridge Mountains with their subjects, the raccoons, goats, and rabbits that have access to their houses. They speak about their land in an offhand manner, and because my father has no such acreage to take for granted, he doesn't interrupt their conversations. Besides, the tales they tell are factual ones and therefore, to be believed; the story-telling impulse on his side of the family runs to exaggeration and self promotion. Lottie and Rudy visit the mountains often, which my mother says makes the apartment bearable. To me, it simply means that my aunt and uncle are not tied down to the maintenance and repair of faulty gutters and loose bricks.

My mother is the last to dress for the party, and will not go upstairs to change until the angel has been mended. Where the wing joins the body, there's a thick line of dark glue; the wooden figure has been repaired and rebroken many times over the years, pushed off the piano, toppled from the tree. My mother cooked up a big pot of glue on the back burner of the stove, anticipating further mishaps to the Christmas decorations.

Lottie came early to help, settling Rudy into a corner of the living room with a beer. She donned an apron to cover a dress that is always stylishly longer or shorter than her sister's and slipped off her heels; I have never seen my aunt wear low shoes, even to the beach. The two sisters work side by side at the sink, one preferring to wash and the other to dry the glasses. While Lottie is partial to the center of the bread loaf, my mother prefers the ends; "rumpftles," she calls them. Lottie rinses her hair a lively shade of red. My mother resigns herself to the grey that has appeared as two wings at her temples. "Kleine," or "Little One," is the nickname of the shorter sister, Sabine, who has difficulty keeping her weight down. Lottie is "Grosse," which refers not to size, but to age.

The two gossip as they work. They are not very discreet and often do this in front of my sister and me. It's understood nothing will go further. Occasionally they counsel one another to leave their husbands. It's out of the question, of course; how could my mother manage with two girls? Lottie never can bring herself to say anything against her brother-in-law. "Gus will keep you tight." That part is true. My father is a decent provider. My mother says she should have heeded the clues. Or not misread them. He had put $20 down on a house without consulting her. "I guess that means we have to get married," he said by way of a proposal. The closer she came to her wedding date, my mother told Lottie, the stranger the rooms in that house looked even with her piano and rug moved in.

It's from these conversations that I'm beginning to understand the ins and outs of married life.

The sisters worry about Hans, who was late coming down from Scarsdale and had recently recovered from a bout of food poisoning. They also worry about the egg man going out of business and, in the same breath, their investments, which make all things possible; Lottie lent her sister some money to put in the stock market. They ponder the latest advice from their deceased stockbroker, Mr. Stern, whose tips are communicated via the ouija board. "Tap twice for yes," Lottie instructs, and rattles off the names of major corporations, mostly those dealing in steel or oil. It's thanks to Mr. Stern that she was able to buy the Studebaker. They laughed again at the thought of their friend, Else, who, calling upon her dead husband, nearly had a heart attack herself as the table under the board slowly rose in the air. When Else asked if he was able to get any schnapps up there, the table came crashing down. "Next," and here my mother covered her face with a dishtowel, ashamed at making a joke at a poor widow's expense, "she'll be wanting to know about the women." "In that case," Lottie said, "she should be addressing the floor instead of the ceiling."

Recently, Lottie has been branching out, having been introduced to the concept of automatic writing by the Baroness von Thyssen. The Baroness' connections are impeccable; she knows the Queen of Spain and her son personally. Since the death of the Baron, she has been reduced to giving singing lessons to pay the rent on her Riverside Drive apartment. Lottie is one of her pupils.

Suddenly, there are boxes at the opera. And recitals at Carnegie Hall, although Lottie has not yet been invited as an active participant. Sometimes she's pressed into service as a page turner or usher, sometimes as an extra woman at dances at the Waldorf-Astoria where there are always more men. To these Lottie wears the velvet cape with the embroidered hood and matching mittens that I covet. On the rare occasions when Rudy attends these events as her escort, Lottie enjoys showing off how well he looks in his handsome evening clothes. That's the reason, my mother maintains, that her sister married him.

When the singing lessons and the parlor games no longer amuse her, Lottie runs away to sea.

I hear my aunt in the kitchen now, practicing scales, warming up. That means the entertainment is about to begin, the moment when my mother's side of the family makes fools of themselves in front of the other relatives. Uncle Hans has finally arrived and is unpacking his violin from its case and setting up the music stand. I'm hungry, his manner suggests, and I want to get this over with.

Lottie peers through the curtains of the French doors, inspecting her audience. Her ear clips are off but she has them back on when she steps out. My father, who was downstairs moving around his gardening pots, is called. Hans takes up his position beside the piano. My mother, fresh from the steamy kitchen, dabs at her nose with a paper napkin and then stuffs it under the cushion of the piano bench.

Lottie pauses a few moments before beginning and I wonder if the Baroness taught her that. Her hands are folded and brought up under her chin; the elbows stick out, ready to begin flapping. Slowly she raises her eyes from beneath the dark brows. As she exhales, the song begins.

Lottie sings from the throat, all the threads in her neck working. Once in awhile she claps her hands for emphasis. Mostly she leans towards the audience, pleading.

For the most part, it's awful. The piano needs tuning. The violin, in spite of the efforts of Hans, who is the most accomplished of the trio, is no match for the singer's vibrato.

For all she knows, my aunt performs alone. I think that the sounds coming from her mouth must be disheartening, so far from the ideal in her head. But she is clearly enjoying herself. Lottie trills not of the war, not of the flight to East Prussia for food, nor the parents left behind. She sings about eating herself full, and the pleasures of making music and wearing pretty clothes. For one moment at least, and here she takes a deep breath and makes a run to a more challenging octave, they celebrate the cultured life.

Hans holds the tempo to his older sister, retreating in the background when Lottie reaches for the highest notes; the moment is all hers. She turns to him as if to say, "Watch me here, this is where it gets tricky." It is a peculiar rendition and singular interpretation, one undreamt of by the composer. Hans slows down to keep pace with my mother, who, alone of the three, is self taught, having run out of money to pay for lessons after she finished paying for the piano. It's because of this habit of accommodation that my father implies that Hans is "weak" and why his wife was able to wrest control of his two sons from him. When my mother drags behind for several bars, Hans moves his foot towards hers on the pedal, urging her to go faster, filling in with extra notes.

Hans started out working as a baker so there would always be bread to eat, but no longer wants to walk the wooden planks among the basement rats. At the big finale, he forgets he is now a paperhanger and probably will always remain so, and guides the music to its crescendo.

When Lottie finishes, she stands erect, if out of breath. No one dares laugh; they are all stunned into silence. I wonder where my aunt has learned that self confidence. That, too, from the Baroness? Why doesn't my mother possess it? More importantly, why don't I?

Lottie inclines her head towards her accompanists, eliciting applause on their behalf and indicating it's their turn in the limelight. My mother and Hans play Fritz Kreisler melodies; no one dances.

When they are finished, it's cousin Margarete's turn. She renders "Malagueña" flawlessly. It's no wonder; she's been playing the same piece for two years now. My mother begs me to demonstrate what I've learned, but I refuse. No one could follow such passionate banging. And I know that whatever music I choose will meet with my father's disapproval. He is never asked to play, but sits down, unbidden, improvising "Tales From the Vienna Woods," adding more notes than are called for and thumping on the pedal to hide those he misses.

When the concert is over, Rudy stands as if on cue. He

threads his way through the makeshift rows of drawn up chairs and walks past me on his way to the bathroom. He touches my head as he climbs the steps, a caress, or perhaps merely to steady himself. I notice the large yellow toenail on his right foot poking through the black silk sock.

At his approach, the bathroom door slams shut and then the door to my bedroom. I hear giggles, a scurrying of cousins, followed by silence. At my mother's direction, the children had gone upstairs, after playing outside, to rummage through my closet for something dry to wear. Charlotte is up there in our room taking off her clothes along with the rest of them.

The only other bedroom was turned into a kitchen to accommodate my father's oldest sister, Hedwig, and her husband when they lived with us and later, Rudy and Lottie for a short, happy time. It has never been transformed back. My mother says she will put a skirt around the sink but neither my sister nor I want to entertain our friends in a room that looks as if, at any moment, serious cooking might go on. Besides, impressive cracks mar the walls so that in places the lathe shows through the plaster and my father is not anxious to fix them. He's counting on one of us getting married and solving the problem. Since Charlotte is two years older, she'll have to go first.

In the meantime, we draw lines down the center of the bed we are forced to share. During the night this boundary is redrawn by wayward arms and legs. In the morning each of us clings to her side, afraid of being caught over the line. Sometimes the trespass is intentional, an excuse to continue an argument. When my father hears us yelling, he charges up the stairs, his slipper raised. Charlotte sleeps closest to the door and feels the full brunt of his anger; lately, she just rolls over and turns up her bottom while I squirm in the farthest corner of the bed. It never hurts, which is a surprise; I always think he's going to kill us.

He said nothing when the cousins were outside stealing the Christmas bulbs off the neighbors' bushes. I, myself, had pocketed about a dozen earlier in the day.

When we started out in the late afternoon, it was still light, and not so cold. Cousin Frieda dragged her sled over the patches of ice on the road to the incineration plant. The garbage overflowed out the plant doors that are always open; inside, the refuse is sorted into two large piles that reach almost to the roof. A thick liquid seeps into the surrounding fields and it was on this frozen substance that we attempted to skate. In the warmer months we stay away from the stuff; you can't get the smell out of your clothes and our mothers are expert at sniffing us out.

We fashioned skates from cardboard or bits of wood which we tied to our shoes with cloth ropes. I wore a pair of boots with leather soles that Lottie had brought back from South America. Lined with shearling, they're too small, and my mother insisted I wear heavy socks; down where my toes were supposed to be, I felt nothing.

It didn't look promising. Wolfie led the way in the growing dark, waving his flashlight on the ground ahead, stomping and testing. There was no real danger except, perhaps, from his mother's wrath. Even though he's a full head taller and too big to put over her knee, Hedwig wouldn't hesitate to take the belt to him.

The tools of Wolfie's taxidermy were still lying on the laundry sink in his basement next to the dirty clothes: a knife and a roll of cotton in a box with a red cross on it. Five birds, sparrows I think, had been propped up stiffly on the drainboard. As he made each cut and then stuffed the tiny cavity, he watched my face. He hadn't suffered my disapproving presence gladly. I'm aware of the differences in our ages, that, although we are related, we come from different families. Among my transgressions, the only one that counts in Wolfie's book is smoking stolen cigarettes behind the billboard near the highway; he considers me an amateur.

"Over here," Wolfie called. We followed like sheep. The ice wasn't thick enough.

"Give it up," Robert said, bored. He hadn't bothered to tie on his skates. I wanted to take a test run with my boots but knew if I broke through the thin crust, I would start the New Year sentenced to a bath and an early bedtime. I began to slide on the road where the snow had been packed down.

Frieda sat on the sled. "Pull me," she said. We all piled on top.

Wolfie and Robert began to wrestle over the possession of the flashlight. There was a sound like someone running fingers over the spokes of a comb. Suddenly our voices seemed too brash, shattering the crisp stillness.

"Sh-h-h-h, listen," said Robert, who had gotten the light away from Wolfie and declared himself as leader.

"Aw, it's just a bird."

We were standing by the only remaining patch of woods. Frieda picked up the sled in her arms and made ready to run.

"This is where the tramps stayed," Charlotte whispered. I thought she was trying to scare Frieda. "When they saw me, they pulled out a gun."

Wolfie grumbled, "It was probably a roasting stick," but lowered his voice.

"I tell you, I saw it by the light of the fire," Charlotte insisted. We looked down at the ground but saw only our footprints. We tiptoed past the alleged site of the camp, then scattered, hightailing it for home, leaving Frieda, who wouldn't abandon her sled, far behind.

We reassembled at the top of the hill which ran down into the alley behind the house. The boys set about building up the sparse icy foundation, carting the snow from greater and greater distances, then running the hose from the laundry tub out the basement window and aiming it over the wall. "Tomorrow, this will be perfect." We jumped onto the slush, packing it down. Frieda was disappointed; she wanted to go sledding now. Her face had turned pale but a bright spot appeared on each cheek. "You don't look well," her brother said, urging her to go inside. "Tante will give you some hot chocolate." I was surprised she gave up so easily, but soon my father's face appeared at the dining room windows. When he saw who it was, Wolfie threw an ice ball against the glass. My father raised his arm but it was a mock fist he made because Wolfie was the one he always took fishing. I thought, it's a good thing that wasn't me.

The goldfish pond with its little marble bench is visible from the dining room windows. In better weather, the bench is a fine place to sit; I can get the fish to eat right out of my hand. The pond is now covered with boards. My father stuffs straw in the cracks to keep out the cold. I thought this also kept out the food, the insects, but in spring there are always a new crop of fingerlings. From that same window my father throws water at any cat that dares enter his garden; he's a protector of all things small and helpless, but I'm going to be fourteen years old.

My father never knew I had pushed a boy off the back wall last spring. He appeared in the middle of the school year and lived with the family on the opposite corner. He had something defective and tentative about him. It was understood he could be sent back from wherever he came at a moment's notice. I showed no mercy, and pushed him just as he was peering over the wall and judging the distance down. Actually, he must have jumped, or so I told myself later. He sustained no injuries, just stared up at me with a look of resignation on his face. I never saw him after that, not even in school.

It wasn't the first time I sensed a potential victim. Edward came under our roof, and my mother's care, when he was three, after his father had abandoned the family. He spent the days with us while his grandmother and mother both worked, and returned to his own home in the evenings. Charlotte and I cut Edward's hair in a particularly savage manner and lathered his face with shaving soap until he howled when it got into his eyes. We played house and he was the baby, confined to a makeshift crib, a playpen, and later, the bathroom. He was five years old and still cried for his mother and grandmother even after we had grown weary of taunting him.

My mother now appeared at the window, nervously motioning us inside. We hung back, huddling just beyond the circle of light thrown down by the streetlamp.

"We better go in," Charlotte said.

Before we were allowed upstairs, we had to go through the laundry room. My mother filled pails with cold water for us to soak our feet in; when I complained, she said, "I told you not to wear those boots," while trying to rub life into my feet with a scratchy towel. She hung up our mufflers, hats and mittens

on the boiler and stuffed our boots with newspapers. Satisfied
that she had put us right again, she returned to her guests.

The concert over, we can now eat. Everyone, that is, except
Rudy, who just shakes his head. Lottie ferries plates of food
for him to inspect. "Just a little something," she begs. The
local butcher shop has been emptied of all its special "wursts."
Along with Hedwig's potato salad there is herring in capers
and vinegar, some other fish in sour cream and onions, five different kinds of bread and rolls and three different varieties of
pickles. And beer and wine, of course. The bottles of scotch
and rye will make their appearance closer to the New Year,
alongside the pot of coffee. My father pours directly from
these bottles even though we own a set of labeled decanters.
The men give each other whiskey as presents, which is what
they most wish to receive themselves. Over the holidays the
liquor cabinet is full, mostly rye. The first drink we children
are allowed is seven and seven.

When it's almost midnight, Robert and Wolfie fight over
the old bugle, and take turns blasting the neighbors. The rest
of the cousins add a few more dents to my mother's pots and
pans, which they bang with mixing spoons. Margarete clangs
two pie plates together. The adults kiss one another on the
lips. Kissing has little to do with affection and is expected by
way of a greeting; for some of the uncles, I suspect it might
be something more, so I stay out of their reach. We don't hug
in our family. Hugging is nicer, an escape into another's arms,
something about which I have been thinking a lot lately.

Everyone is called for coffee and cake. The tablecloths
have been changed and new napkins brought out; my mother's

been ironing for days. The cakes are cut into. Again, each aunt has provided her specialty. For the uncles, for my father, these are never as good as those baked by their mothers, when the family cow produced the milk for the butter and the pet chickens the eggs. I grasp sugar cubes with the silver tongs and stack them on my plate around a piece of each kind of cake, then dunk the cubes into the coffee and suck them one by one. I drop a dollop of whipping cream into the hot liquid and another onto a piece of nut cake. Hedwig gives me a disapproving look; it's her opinion the cake doesn't need embellishment. Rudy takes no interest in the desserts whatsoever; he's moved back into his corner, intent on his beer. He hasn't graduated to the schnapps, the way my father has; he doesn't go to bars, the way his brother-in-law does. But my father doesn't get drunk at home.

Going to bars is serious. There, my father and uncles can blame the Depression, or their bosses, sometimes even their wives for their misfortunes. The wives stay at home and complain about the disappearance of the providers. Drinking in bars nurtures a feeling of regret; this leads, in turn, to the drinking up of paychecks and letting the house go. My mother struggles to do what she can, touching up the walls with paint, moving the furniture to cover the worst cracks, but my father is the mason in the family.

As long as there are so many uncles with so many specialties, my father knows that, eventually, whatever needs to be repaired, will be. We have been waiting for weeks for the carpenter, uncle Joaquin, to come down from the Bronx to fix the broken basement step. In the meantime, my mother put a chair in front of the stairs to remind us children not to plunge headlong down them two at a time.

. . .

The evening is over. Lottie and Rudy are always the first to leave because, in the absence of the bus at such a late hour, they have a subway to catch. (The car is reserved for long trips since finding a place to park in front of their apartment building is difficult and so, once claimed, not easily abandoned.) I shake hands with Rudy. I kiss my aunt. Lottie suddenly hugs me. I bury my nose in the collar of her fur coat.

This is a stylish couple. Rudy wears a brown felt fedora; the grosgrain ribbon has been lost long ago. The camelhair coat is belted and he has worn it for all the years I have known him. The cuffs are frayed, the lining is worn, although the seams have been redone many times with Lottie's precise stitches. She had plenty of practice sewing up the torn pockets on uniforms when she followed Rudy from camp to camp. I notice the hem of the coat is coming undone and fear he will catch the heel of his professionally polished shoes in it. He had gone into the bathroom and wet his hair in an attempt to get it to go straight back.

This is more than a matter of grooming. This goes beyond clothing. Beyond jewelry, beyond my aunt's engagement diamond even, considered a formidable stone in these post-Depression times. A certain semblance of a style of life is to be kept up at all costs.

It will be cold walking to the train. They put their arms around one another and gingerly navigate the porch steps; my mother turns on the light. I hope that the wine as well as the coats will warm them. The cousins are gathered up and sent home, some across the street, others down the block, while their parents linger on, talking about how it's too bad my mother is stuck with all the dishes while Lottie is excused and how these holiday celebrations are never scheduled at her apartment. My mother protests that it's too small, that her sister is the most generous person in the world, and plunges her hands into the soapy water.

When my mother was ill and Charlotte and I were help-less to do anything about it, Lottie came and stayed for several days, going from kitchen to phone, administering mustard plasters, calling to see that Rudy was eating. That none of this closeness has rubbed off on her own daughters is painful for my mother, but I figure my sister and I had been divided at birth. Charlotte is fair with large bones and I'm dark; along with her temperament, I have inherited Lottie's build.

All the guests gone, it's time for my father to let the para-keet out of the cage for its exercise. The bird flies madly from corner to corner, delirious in its freedom, coming to rest on the curtain boxes. It swoops down and walks back and forth on the rim of my father's glasses while he reads in his chair.

I have warned my father. My mother and I both cautioned him about leaving the French doors open. I'm afraid of the bird, afraid its little claws on my shoulder will put me into a panic; my mother worries about the mess it will make in the living room.

Someone has left the door leading to the basement open. Perhaps the parakeet senses fresher air, wanting to escape from the smoke-filled rooms. Perhaps it sniffs traces of the garbage from the incineration plant on our wet clothing, the rotting seeds. "Catch him," my father says, lunging after the bird and knocking over the chair in front of the stairs. He hits the light switch. My mother, sure he is going to trip on the loose step, urges him to slow down. I imagine the water bugs scuttling back into the dark corners and realize I have no shoes on. "Stay back," my father warns, "you'll get him excited." I can hear the bird flapping its wings from one corner of the basement to the other. The door to the boiler room is open; my father asks if anyone bothered to close the back door when they came inside. He turns on my mother, "You were the last one downstairs with them, weren't you?" "No!" I raise my voice to my father, but say nothing more by way of explanation when I might have taken the blame onto myself. He edges his way over to the door and as it bangs shut, the bird sails up and over my father's head, past the boiler and the drying scarves and mittens, out the open window where the hose still dangles, into the cold, New Year's air. My father follows, calling. My mother runs after him with his coat. It's useless. My father turns the outside light off and on several times, signaling. We persuade him to wait until morning.

Charlotte thinks we should buy another parakeet. But I know Hansel is irreplaceable in my father's heart; already he's beginning to yearn. As he climbs the stairs, his face takes on a wistful expression. There will never be another such bird, capable of repeating his own name. There will never be another apple cake as fine tasting as his mother's. My father pours a short one, settles himself on the piano bench, easing into the first bars of the "Emperor's Waltz." I long to sit beside him, to point out that, after all, he still has us, but I'm my mother's daughter, and a coward.

It will be some time yet, but that time will come, when not even the thought of his missed dinner will coax my father off the bar stool. Either my mother or I will have to retrieve him, force his arms into the jacket sleeves, guide him to the door, and point him in the direction of home.

BIG AND LITTLE

2

The first journey, measured in geographic distance, was the shortest. Only an inch or so on the map to the Prussian border, no more than the length from the tip of Papa's forefinger to his knuckle. He touched the end of Sabine's nose.

"It's only for three months."

To a child of seven, a summer can seem interminable, especially if your mother is awaiting another baby sure to usurp your position in the family as its darling. Her older sister, Lottie, tasted the words, "East Prussia," and found their strangeness appealing.

"Think of the extra flour and cheese we could send home. After we've eaten our fill. All we want," she said, scarcely believing it herself. Sabine was not persuaded.

The city was empty of young men, off somewhere fighting. This was what the children knew of the war. The songs their father played on the violin were melancholy tunes. Ceremonies had turned into frugal affairs, seldom calling for a hired musician. Materials for the cigars he made to supplement the family income were hard to come by; still in shorter supply were the customers. The wives of the cigar smokers stopped requesting the elaborate handwork which was their mother's specialty. It was just as well; Emilia was sewing little in her present, weakened condition and could not even keep down the pigeon soup she craved. Already she had been to the cemetery to see that everything was in order. With the last of the flour, she made pancakes as if there was something to celebrate.

The friends and relatives arrived with long faces, hoping to be remembered at harvest time. Lottie was squeezed and kissed, tickled by the moustaches of old women, who swore she was like one of their own, which gave them the right to carry on. They had behaved almost as outrageously when Hans was apprenticed to the baker in the next town. Sabine, seeing all the attention lavished on her older sister, decided at the last moment that she would not be left behind. But Suzanne, her doll, must accompany them, along with the doll's extensive wardrobe, sewn by mother.

"Tell her she can take the thing," father said, turning away.

In the morning there was a rush to pack the children's belongings and Suzanne's clothes, which fit into a little trunk of their own. The girls were dressed in their Sunday aprons and skirts, their boots shined; the people of East Prussia were to know from what sort of family they came. Emilia twisted Sabine's hair around her wrist, then abruptly turned over the brush to Lottie, who fought to catch the ends of the braid in the ribbon.

"Not so hard," her mother instructed, attempting to guide her daughter's impatient hands.

"Maybe you shouldn't accompany us," her husband advised; outside the wind twisted the sheets on the line.

"I have more than enough ballast to keep from being blown over," Emilia answered, filling her cheeks with air, arms extended out from her sides for balance. The girls had to laugh at that.

They walked to the train station, or rather were pushed along, their mother secure between them. The upstairs neighbor trudged behind with the suitcases, the wind blowing dust into his eyes; those were not tears. The weather was bound to be better in East Prussia, their father promised.

On the platform, Lottie recited her absentminded good-byes, innocently assuming that when she and her parents met again they would be unchanged except, of course, that her mother would be thinner. She'd seen Gretel, a friend, and hurried away.

"Come on Kleine," Lottie called, boarding the train, leaving her parents to memorize the slender contours of their daughter's back. Sabine was pried from her father's shoulder where she had flung herself; he had been kneeling, pressing food into her hands for the trip. The neighbor, forgotten in the rush, threw the suitcases up into the car.

"The time will go quickly," their father said, his knees giving way. He clung to his wife. With one hand she waved; with the other she held her belly, imagining all of her children well fed.

Sabine stood on the seat with her face pressed against the glass. Almost immediately the train entered a tunnel and her parents were lost to her sight, she believed, forever. Lottie had to coax her sister down onto her lap. She had already begun to imagine their new family. She was more curious than afraid. It was not that Lottie was unaware of danger. She knew in what uniform it clothed itself. But surely not even the Russians would harm children.

Finally, Sabine's sniffling deteriorated into the occasional ragged hiccough. She dressed Suzanne for lunch. Lottie undid the parcel of food. As a treat, along with the bacon fat sandwiches, there were lightly buttered pieces of caraway bread sprinkled with sugar, a half for each, which they ate immediately. They slept for awhile, the younger's head bumping and falling off her sister's shoulder with each fitful halt and start of the train which skirted the edges of the larger towns, then ran through the center of small villages. The interval between stops increased as the landscape opened out into fields, some cultivated, most untilled. Empty except for the scavenging birds.

The sisters had been warned to remain seated and together; the car was to be uncoupled and picked up by another engine further down the line. From inside the next compartment came muffled laughter, then a banging noise as if someone were being pitched against the wall. Lottie heard running in the corridor, Gretel's high-pitched challenge, the answering shout of a boy.

"Get off me," Lottie said, waking her sister. When she peered out to investigate, all was still. She yanked Sabine by the arm into the aisle. Suddenly a whistle sounded and the girls found themselves pushed back inside the next compartment, the door locked behind them. The train was slowing, approaching the border. Curious, Lottie looked out; there was Gretel waving from the next window. The two motioned to each other over the noise.

"Look at what I found," Sabine said importantly. On the seat in a covered basket lay a cake, its layers adhered with vanilla cream, pristine except where someone had run a finger around the edge. Gretel's mother hoped the sweet bribe would buy a measure of tolerance for her impetuous daughter. It had been a long time since the girls had seen anything so wonderful.

"Over here, Gretel," Lottie taunted, "we're going to eat your cake." The girl shrieked in protest. The train had come to a stop. It was easy enough for her to climb out of the window, but to reach her friends she had to grasp the hooks on the outside of the car; these were spaced far apart, and her progress was slow.

"Go back," Lottie warned, but this was not possible. The train lurched, then moved forward. Sabine rattled the doorknob, frantically trying to get out, to get help, to escape before the punishment, which was sure to follow, would rain down on their heads. Thwarted, she sat on the floor and wailed. Gretel was going to be killed, along with her sister; Lottie was hanging out of the window and all Sabine could see were the backs of her sister's legs.

"Hold on to me," Lottie commanded, "I'm going to catch Gretel's hands." Sabine did not move. Lottie fell backwards, Gretel tumbling after her. Righting herself, Gretel began to laugh.

"What a brave girl," Lottie said, with admiration, brushing at her friend's skirts.

"You lied to me about the cake," Gretel said, inspecting the basket. "I pulled that fool stunt for nothing." But what a story she had to tell! She began to recount her adventure, exaggerating the danger, her cheeks flushed. Sabine wished the two would be still; someone might hear. Now they were going to get it, but no grownups appeared. Mysteriously, the door had been unlocked. Apparently, there was to be no retribution; they had taken a risk and were to get off unscathed. Her older sister had lost all reason and was now encouraging Gretel to eat the cake. Nothing made sense anymore to the little girl who sat in a cowardly heap on the floor. The world was a perilous place and she had been lured from home into it.

The train sat in wait at a siding for the relief engine; it was early evening by the time they approached their destination. Beyond the darkening fields the children could see the outlines of what appeared to be mountains, blue and glowing. A series of small fires were consuming the trees on the ridge; like the fiery spines of a dragon, Sabine thought. Just below, a house was tucked into a notch of one of the foothills, its windows alight, as if the fire had managed to get inside.

Among the strangers waiting for them was an elderly bear of a man who seemed to be in charge; the others referred to him simply as "Judge." He called out the names of the children and from the anonymous group assembled on the train platform one eager woman after another stepped forward. Sabine stared dumbly at the hills; no one appeared concerned.

The large man said, "They're only burning off slash, but it's a pretty sight, isn't it?" If he were to claim them, Sabine decided, it wouldn't be so bad. But when two women approached Lottie, she hung back. It was difficult to see the faces, their brows bound in scarves. The tall one, whose bony wrists dangled from her sleeves, seemed to defer to the older woman who wore a pair of man's boots. They had bargained for only one child. Lottie pleaded, pushing a scrawny Sabine forward.

"My sister's a good worker," she said. She had instructed her charge to keep her mouth shut and, above all, not to cry.

In the morning, when father did not tickle them awake, even Lottie had difficulty holding back the tears. They peered from under the covers at the rude attic space. They had slept badly on the straw mattress and the hard, unyielding limbs of Suzanne had come between them.

"Get up," Lottie prodded. "From now on, if we want something to eat, we're going to have to make it ourselves."

The girls sat in what they took to be the kitchen and stared, too shy to investigate. Berenice, who had been up for hours, slipped away from her chores and her mother-in-law's scrutiny and made each of the children an egg on a piece of bread which they ate hungrily. Lottie marveled at how the young woman managed not to break the yolk; Berenice was taken aback at their request for a knife and fork. She pushed the hair back under her cap as she spoke, then impatiently pulled its ties from under her chin and flung it down on the table. Both hands were now free to paint a picture for them of how her life would be when her husband returned from the war.

"We have a lot of catching up to do." Berenice blushed. Then, almost apologetically, she ushered them outside to introduce them to their chores.

In the following days, Sabine found that she could not do even the simplest tasks without vexing one or the other woman and sometimes, her own sister, who soon grew tired of her continual questioning. Set to fetching the water, she could manage only one bucket at a time; someone had to help her prime the pump. Sabine learned to be silent, to make herself as small as possible, wished she might become invisible, especially to Anna, who flushed her out from where she hid among the cool shadows of the well house. Sabine feared this large-bosomed woman who threw herself down on the earth to pray; even while milking, Anna worked her lips in silent chant.

Lottie much preferred to be inside, on her own to do the mending, or make the butter, to prepare the vegetables for their simple meals; to Berenice she left the plucking of the chickens. She learned to reduce the flour, butter and water, stirring continuously so the mixture wouldn't burn; this was the base for the gravy that sauced the geese Anna slaughtered. Each morning Lottie took inventory, tallying the riches. In addition to the flour, milk, butter and eggs, there was fruit. She made

a doughy base into which she stuck plums, boiling the dump-
lings and then pouring melted butter over them; it was almost
like eating cake. They never did send any wheat home. They
had forgotten what it felt like to be hungry. Lottie, believing that Sabine was not doing her share of the work, could
not bring herself to broach the subject. Mother wasn't eating
much now anyway.

At night, in bed together, Sabine felt her sister returned
to her. They made fun of the uneducated dialect in which
the women spoke, Berenice's constant chatter about her absent
husband, the fact that the chickens had the run of the front
room. Lottie stuffed a pillow under her nightshirt in imitation of Anna and prostrated herself on the floor while saying
her prayers.

At the judge's house, the floors were carpeted in rugs,
unlike the dirt floor of the farmhouse. A room had been set
aside specifically for the purpose of bathing inside the house,
complete with tub. Gretel boasted about the wonders of her
life with the village's leading citizen. Reunited each day for
a few hours in a makeshift classroom, the children compared
experiences. The teacher, a young woman barely out of school
herself and ill equipped to deal with so many homesick, foreign
children, had not learned to resort to threats. She had lived
in the village all of her life and what she knew of the remote
world, she feared. The children sensed this. Gretel was a prime
candidate for discipline, fidgeting in her seat, whispering inces-
santly; the others waited for the familar sounds of the ruler
cutting through air, the smack on the upturned palms. At
the end of the first day when no such punishment was meted
out, the poor teacher lost all control of her pupils, who came
to view their hours in the classroom as a brief holiday from

chores. They had been placed, for the most part, in childless households, the only ones which could afford an additional mouth to feed; at school the lonely exiles greeted each other with loud, excited voices as the dearest of friends.

Harvest brought an end to this reprieve. In the fields there was little opportunity, or energy, for play. Here, the children were more closely supervised. Even so, one or two managed to slip away. Sabine was among those, dropping onto her knees and disappearing amid the rows of corn.

The women then instructed her to watch the geese. Here, surely, was a task she could manage. The birds' wings were clipped. All that was required was to throw them some grain. This accomplished, Sabine settled herself under a tree, suspended an umbrella from its lower branches, and concentrated on her book. Once in awhile she looked up; the geese had spread themselves around the edges of the pond. Even through the umbrella, which cast a shadow across the page, she could feel the warm sun and soon fell asleep. The barn cat, fat and bored, lumbered around the pond, bent on mischief. Suddenly there was a squawking, a few birds sounded a general alarm, which sent the rest fleeing. Sabine woke, saw the flock disperse and wondered which half to pursue. It made no difference; the birds refused to be herded back towards the water. The group of two soon became four; there was nothing to do but admit defeat. Before she could call out to Lottie, Anna, hearing the commotion, came running. She, in turn, shouted for Berenice. Sabine ran off, sure the witch was hard on her heels.

The women searched long after dark, shining their lanterns into the recesses of the well house and the child's usual hiding places. She was lured out of the furthest reaches of the

barn only by the sound of her sister's voice, "Kleine, Kleine."
Sabine made a dash for the sanctuary of Lottie's skirts. She
was too frightened to notice the look of concern on Anna's
face give way to relief.

The judge came to confirm for himself the rumors about
the deplorable conditions under which the children were living.
Lottie was ashamed she had mentioned anything to Gretel,
whom she knew had a gift for exaggeration. The judge satisfied himself they were being well taken care of and was about
to leave, when Anna begged him to take the girls since they
were so obviously unhappy at the farm.

"I've lived so long without children," she said, "I've forgotten how to speak without frightening them."

When the judge could not disengage Sabine from his coat
sleeve, he relented. She waved from the safety of the wagon.

Anna sighed. "See, Berenice, how happy the little one is
to be leaving us."

Lottie told the judge's wife she preferred to bathe herself,
but Sabine welcomed the attention. Even Suzanne got a good
scrubbing so that her hair, once a tumble of curls, stood up
in stiff tufts about her face. The judge's wife was a slight
woman, which reminded the girls of their mother; each kindness Irene bestowed upon them brought on a new flood of
weeping. This only intensified her efforts to protect them;
she kept the children under her watchful eye, inside, like house
pets, and Lottie had far less autonomy in the kitchen than she
had been accustomed to on the farm.

She wondered if Irene's small frame was the result of living
in a house where everything appeared to be in miniature; the
tables and sofas rested on spindly legs. Even the few flowers in

the garden beds were staked upright so their frail stalks would not bend and snap. Perhaps Anna had grown to such formidable size because the farmhouse and fields had given her the space to do so. Lottie thought the judge would surely knock over the china figurines, or bump into the tea cart with its assemblage of gilded cups and saucers, but he moved agilely on slippered feet among the parlor furniture which was at greater risk from Gretel, who wielded the feather duster with a heavy hand.

Given little work to do, Sabine followed Irene until the woman, in self defense, taught the child to crochet. At last the simple repetitions were mastered, if loosely; Sabine was pleased with herself. The only sound in the long afternoons, besides the ticking of the French clocks, was of their mistress' voice, instructing Lottie in the dinner preparations and Sabine in how many stitches to take. Lottie was relieved not to have to look after her sister constantly, but jealous that Sabine did not have to so much as peel a potato, or carry in a stick of wood. She and Gretel plotted against the child, excluding her from their fun, poking at each other with stockinged feet under the dinner table, closing the door when their laughter drew her near. At night, they unraveled the day's hard-earned rows of crocheting.

Summer dragged on long into September. The fires burned on the hillsides until it became dry and dangerous; one day Sabine looked up to see they had been extinguished. The heat rose in waves off the tracks; they shimmered and seemed to disappear before her eyes. How was the train to take them home? But the trains came only at night and were never empty. Through raised windows they heard the wagons rolling back from the Russian front, the wounded ferried in open cars; their groans mingled with the lowing of cows. Irene's husband instructed her to pack the children's things.

"Too damned close," he said.

The suitcases stood poised for flight. In his narrow bed, the judge shivered.

3

To be recognized by the waiters as a cook--one of their own--in spite of the hand creams and fresh coat of bright polish, was humbling. Especially in a place of such style.

Located on New York's Upper East Side, the Continental Café aspired to the grandeur of its more sophisticated namesakes in Vienna, Budapest and Prague. It declared itself in gold letters on the windows, the tendrils of the baroque "C" infringing on the "O." Through the other vowels a beaded lampshade or bare arm could be glimpsed.

The waiters pirouetted about with their trays in a desire to impress the patrons, who were, after all, emigrés like themselves, but the moment they opened their mouths, out spilled the country. Lottie had worked on a farm and there was no shame in that. But if one of them touched her sleeve as he set down the pot of chocolate and asked to stand her to a pastry, perhaps even a movie, she always answered with a firm, "No."

The Café was readily accessible by subway, a place where a woman might go by herself on a Sunday, cook's day off, and have coffee and something sweet. But if it should happen that she did not leave alone, meeting at the Continental was as good as an introduction by a trusted friend.

So many delights to choose from behind the glass: the famed Bee Cake--a perfect concoction of nuts, yeast, and honey--marzipan in the shape of acorns or pigs, strawberries infused with cognac. Lottie ordered the Linzertorte because she could not afford to be disappointed, and coming upon the raspberry jam inside the rich crust was always satisfying. If Sabine had been there to order the Bee Cake, they might have shared. But she wouldn't venture out, even when Lottie hinted that someone else might pay. Sabine did not understand this. It must have something to do with America, she reasoned, that people could be so open about their desires and expect them to be fulfilled.

Lately, a note of challenge had entered her voice. "Going along with you, Lottie, is not without its dangers."

Sabine had not forgiven her sister for East Prussia. She insisted that all her travels since that time had been marked by trouble.

After East Prussia, America. Lottie first, Sabine wooed from home a year later. The letters piled up, the evidence of the good life, the most compelling a photograph of her sister standing in front of a house with a sheltering porch, her arms around two girls and a boy, all of them dressed in white, and smiling. Even the boy who liked to kick Lottie in the shins, he, too, was smiling, putting his best face on for the photographer. Sabine never thought to ask if her sister was happy. Lottie never suggested otherwise. As a child, she knew, Sabine would find the kernal of winter in the midst of the balmiest day, triumphantly pull the worm from the apple, content that her direst predictions had come true.

At Ellis Island they gave Sabine white bread and baloney for lunch. "America can't be such a bad place," she thought, "if they put wurst between two pieces of cake."

On the subway, the first black man she had ever seen returned her stares with a scowl. She looked down at her shoes for the rest of the trip. She had not looked up since.

· · ·

A waiter hurried over with a cart before Lottie had a chance to take off her gloves. She pointed to the torte.

"A good choice. My own personal favorite. If there's anything else you should desire…"

She chose to ignore him and settled herself, laying the coat on the opposite chair, taking care not to hide the label, although the lining did appear a bit thin. "The outside still has a good deal of wear in it." That was what Mrs. Stevens had said when she gave her the coat. Lottie was planning to replace the buttons.

Good, two cigarettes were left. There was a trick to lifting one partway to the lips, waiting but appearing not to wait, for a light. Lottie did this several times with no luck. No matter; the third time was always the charm. The waiter arrived, dipped the tray towards her with one hand and with the other deftly lit the cigarette. He set down the whipped cream in its dish off to the side, and the coffee in the pitcher, enough for two cups. Lottie nodded, indicating she would stay awhile, so that he did not drop the check. When he was gone, she tapped out the cigarette, now faintly imprinted with her lipstick, and eased it back under the elastic in the silver case.

This was a good table because it had a clear view of the entrance. Many of the faces were familiar, but she had never seen the group sitting at a nearby table, their backs against the window. The men looked more like boys and two were in uniform. A third had neglected to remove his overcoat even though the air inside the restaurant was close. Lottie would have remembered seeing the woman; there was nothing girlish about her. She inclined her head first to one man, then to another, as if to share equally in their admiration. This creature had managed to roll her hair so tightly that none of the pins showed. Even when Lottie's own hair was long, it had a life of its own and would not have been managed so tidily. She had saved the braid, coiled in a net, in the dresser drawer. Now when she pinned it to the back of her neck, Lottie saw that its color was innocently dark; America had made her a redhead.

What the woman needed were tortoise shell barrettes in the midst of all that blondeness. In a splendid place like this, one required a gimmick. Something Sabine didn't understand.

"Once again, you've gone too far," she had said, spitting on her handkerchief and wiping the dark spot of pencil from beside her sister's mouth.

Raising the fork to her lips, Lottie broke off a bit of the torte crust, putting the fork down after each bite; if properly done, she could make it last for half an hour. She sipped the coffee slowly, so as not to appear greedy for the heady mix of fresh cream and dark liquor. But not so slowly as to be suspected of lingering when her table might better host someone with a fatter wallet. There was still the second cup and she could always stand herself to another pot. After all, the cream, which was whipped with vanilla and sugar, was free and almost as good as the pastry. And then still more sugar in the coffee, two lumps, if only for the pleasure of using the tongs with their tiny silver digits.

Cooks and soldiers, all of them off duty. The trio was making ready to leave; perhaps that was why the one man had his coat on. The woman with the elegant head tried to detain him, grabbing at his lapels, but he was too quick and dodged her embrace. As he left, he bumped the chair on which Lottie's coat rested, and it slid to the floor.

His eyes were the same color as his hair, the color, she would swear later, of caramels. Was it possible to read something there other than politeness? With what diligence he settled the garment back onto its perch, how gracefully the bending down and straightening up were accomplished.

Over the shoulders of his own coat, which was belted like a bathrobe, a fringed scarf was tossed as an afterthought. He gave a little salute, either "sorry" or "goodbye," she couldn't tell which, and was gone. Lottie could see his friends outside, impatiently tapping on the glass and motioning. No doubt they were late for some party. He had brushed her head with his sleeve; surely, no accident.

In three swift bites the dessert was eaten; there was still half a cup of coffee left in the pot. Tenderly, she gathered up the coat. The Café suddenly seemed lifeless, as if a current had been discharged in the air, relieving it of all tension.

The subway ride had a sobering effect. The car was almost empty except for a man who sat with his back towards Lottie; unlike Sabine, she had learned not to take these things personally. A child came running on stubby legs; she expected an adult to follow, but none appeared. He opened the door to the next car with some difficulty and was swallowed up in the noise. She was grateful for all the space in which to examine how sorry she was feeling for herself; tomorrow there was to be a dinner party and Mr. Stevens would follow hard on Lottie's heels making clipped, sarcastic comments about her food. She could say a thing or two to him, but he had taken German in high school.

Sabine was eager to hear it all. The sisters sat on their shared bed. "Don't leave anything out."

Lottie was unusually reticent. She offered half of the lipstick-stained cigarette, but Sabine didn't like the smell. Oddly enough she tolerated, even enjoyed, cigars because it reminded her of home and those father made. The child had glued strips of blue velvet into the wooden boxes. The wood came from Indonesia, the tobacco was imported, even the hinges were of foreign manufacture. Father complained that the family income was at the mercy of every politician's whim.

Sabine was keeping company now with a man who also preferred cigars, but Gus was addicted to the cheaper variety, although Lottie suspected he wouldn't turn down a more expensive one if it were offered. Sabine met Gus' mother on board ship; the old matchmaker stuck close, knowing a good prospect when she saw one.

Not that her son wasn't handsome in an offhand careless way, Lottie had to admit that, but he did take himself too seriously. Even Sabine didn't dare tease him. But then, she didn't often try. The notion that she and Gus might chatter and gossip among themselves like friends seemed odd; after all, that's what sisters were for.

Lottie had observed that, even in traffic, Gus never took Sabine's arm. And he talked too freely about his previous acquaintances, especially a woman who was "in the theatre business." She also knew that Gus' sisters cooked his meals and ironed his shirts and that their husbands were eager to see someone else assume that responsibility.

Sabine agreed that marriage was nothing to be entered into lightly, but lately Lottie had begun to notice some backsliding. Didn't they have Hans' quick, unhappy union as a warning? No one, least of all the groom, had understood a word of the Russian Orthodox ceremony.

"Our brother doesn't know what he's getting himself into," Lottie whispered.

Of the Ukrainian bride, Sabine had only said, "I don't trust that one."

To Lottie's surprise, Sabine offered to accompany her to the Café the following week. She must be dissuaded--would the man even approach their table with two of them sitting there? But how selfish she was to deprive her sister of such a simple pleasure. Lottie confessed everything. Only for a moment did Sabine display disappointment, then quickly brightened, "Oh, now," she said, "you'll have someone, too."

Perhaps the man had been a stranger to the Café. He was probably a soldier and even now was back at his camp. Whenever Lottie voiced these sentiments, Sabine was encouraging.

"It's worth a try. What can you lose?"

She had embroidered a medallion of gold and silver threads onto a plain felt hat and surprised Lottie as she went out the door. Not before cautioning, however, "Don't get your hopes up."

"You're the best sister," Lottie said, pinning the hat into place, "even if you are the gloomiest. What will you do this afternoon?"

"I'll go to the movies." This was a lie. Sabine felt stupid, unable to make out what the people on the screen were saying.

"Why don't you invite Alex, that Greek from your citizenship class? Choose an English film. You both could use the practice."

Sabine didn't wish to encourage the man, who sat unattractively squeezed into the child's desk adjoining hers. Lottie pressed her sister to become a citizen, but Sabine was uncertain of taking such a final, possibly fatal, step. To her, language class was just another form of school to be feared.

Since coming to America she was always being forced to learn something new. On her first day of work, Mrs. Stevens grilled her relentlessly in English about her duties. Sabine merely shook her head, "Yes." The woman then asked whether she understood what was required of her. She shook her head, "No." When Mrs. Stevens raised her hand in frustration, Sabine flinched, expecting to hear the sound of the ruler cut through air.

The sisters were to go to Niagara Falls for three days, their first vacation from work. They had missed the train, which left from Penn Station. Sabine sat on her bag in the middle of Grand Central, and wailed, "I can't go back, I won't," leaving her sister to pick up her clothes and make the necessary excuses. Mr. Stevens had plenty to say about that.

"I'm always getting you out of scrapes," Lottie complained. "Not true," Sabine countered, "You're always getting me into them."

Now she worked for a widower with two small children. Lottie was afraid her sister's interest in Gus had less to do with his charms and more to do with the fact that her employer was coming close to the end of his period of mourning. In the evenings, walking back to their place, Sabine passed the apartments below sidewalk level relegated to the building superintendents, and admired the smug lights in the barred windows.

"I'd like to live there alone and not be bossed around."

"You'll have to get your papers first," Lottie said, stretching the truth.

. . .

Entering the Café, Lottie clutched her refurbished hat. Today, they wouldn't dare hurry along someone so well dressed. The man was there; she saw him through the window and took longer than usual sizing up the choices in the case. He came up behind her.

"The hearts are good," he offered, his voice at her ear. "Are you fond of chocolate?" She thought she would gladly tell him all of her likes and dislikes. When she pointed to the torte and the woman had taken it out and placed it on its doily, he said in the precise, hesitant tone of someone whose struggles with the language were not yet over, "Won't you allow me?" and extended a bill.

"Thank you," she replied first in English and then, turning to face her benefactor, "You are kind," in German.

Without the bulk of his coat and scarf, he seemed less intimidating. But, once seated, talk did not come easily, certainly not as it had when he spoke with his friends. He was flexing his fingers, shaping a little temple with his hands; Lottie could only stare at the hollow space they made to avoid his eyes. The knuckles on her own hands were coarse, and she kept them in her lap. He had set his coat on top of hers, as if moving in.

"Tell me," he asked, "how many make up your household?" He fidgeted, raking his fingers through his straight hair. He needed a haircut. She thought she could do that.

"There are two of us, my younger sister and I." He really was attractive, she decided, even though it looked as if his nose had been broken at one time.

"Ah, two such as you." He sounded as if he couldn't believe his luck.

Shifting his weight in the chair, he stretched his legs and then retracted them when a waiter came by. Lottie sensed his discomfort, and worried that, at any moment, he would stand up, and excuse himself.

Sabine would demand an accounting, so details were important. But she could scarcely tell her sister that when he leaned over and rubbed the beauty mark off her face, it seemed the most natural gesture in the world.

There was little conversation to relate, which was fine with Lottie; she didn't think you learned much about people by what they chose to tell you. When he suggested they take a walk, she welcomed the silence and concentrated on matching her stride to his. He stopped and turned Lottie towards him, pulling the collar of the coat up around her face.

Today the East River was the color of her mother's unpolished pewter plates. Only when a tugboat's passage broke the dull skin did Lottie feel the water had any dimension at all. She didn't want to think of the river at its ending, of the sea and another boat trip. Her parents continued to hope one day she would have enough of whatever foolishness it was that kept her in America. If their eldest daughter returned home, Sabine was sure to follow.

Rudy insisted he could smell the ocean.

Lottie said, "I believe you."

She felt rich standing there wearing such an original hat and a good coat, with the man's hand over hers on the railing. Rich with the sense of possibility. Lottie was confident she could win him over, less confident she would be given the time.

They met on her days off, Rudy having a less rigid schedule. Sometimes they went to Jones Beach, sometimes up to

Scarsdale to see Hans. They had a table now at the Café that the waiters recognized as "theirs" with a good view of the traffic in front. Often Lottie arrived first, almost giddy with anticipation.

Outside, a woman paced in front of the entrance, stopping to peer more closely at the sidewalk, or bending to straighten a stocking. The back was familiar. Lottie was sure it was the same woman they saw in the lobby of the movie theatre the other evening, although the light had not been the best. Lottie had spent a sleepless night imagining a taller, more finely boned person than the one of average stature standing now in the full afternoon sun. The woman held herself with a strictness that gave the casual skirt and blouse she was wearing a formal look. And those very high heels--Lottie wondered what she did for a living.

She had not been alone in the theatre--perhaps she was waiting for the same gentleman now--and Lottie took that as a good sign. Rudy had barely nodded by way of acknowledgment. He did say, offhandedly, "I think that's my wife," as if they were still united. The woman had not appeared to notice him. Lottie was convinced, while waiting in vain for sleep to overtake her that night, she still loved him. Who wouldn't?

"Why torture yourself?" Sabine asked. "The less known about that subject, the better." It was the first time Lottie could remember being enamored with such uncomfortable consequences. There had been other suitors, of course, but she was always careful to keep the balance of affection in her favor.

She had met Hal on the ship coming over the second time after visiting her parents. He was an engineer with artistic ambitions and Lottie was quite willing to nudge him in that direction. It was Hal who gave her the cigarette case. They saw each other constantly for over a year, always with Sabine in tow, during which time Lottie helped him bring over his sisters. That proved to be a mistake. Shortly after they were settled in, Hal became reacquainted with one of their school friends, a woman from the same town, and decided to become an engineer after all. Well, he was a provincial fellow, like her mother's neighbors who marveled at Lottie's clothes as they hung on the line, and wondered at her shoes with their holes in the toes and the open backs. In Hal's case, it was easy enough to convince herself that she missed not his company but their outings in his jaunty car. Some day, she vowed, she was going to learn to drive herself.

But this ex-wife business was something of a shock. The subject of a former marriage might not come up in idle conversation, but their discussions lately seemed headed in a more serious direction. Until that moment, Lottie had been content just to be in Rudy's company. She was in no hurry and had been careful never to inquire after the exquisitively-coiffed blonde. But the knowledge that someone else had played such an important part in his life was a bit unnerving and a reminder that Lottie might not fit into his future plans. Rudy was going away soon. "It's in the works," he said, referring to his tentative standing in the military. She had never seen him in uniform, unlike his friends. At one point, Lottie sensed a falling out with them and, after that time, she had him all to herself. Except on those occasions when Gus had to work and Sabine was a reluctant chaperone. Lottie had been urging her sister, not without some guilt, to see Alex.

Today, impatient, eager to be out in the spring air, she decided she would greet Rudy as he emerged from the subway.

But the woman, intent on her pacing, turned directly in Lottie's path as she exited the Café; it would be rude not to extend some greeting.

"Excuse me," she said. "Rhea, isn't it?"

The woman stepped back. "Do we know each other?" she asked, suspicious, appraising Lottie in her shabby coat, the handmade stitches on the hat.

"Rudy mentioned your name. We saw you in the lobby of the movie theatre. The other evening. It would be only natural... We are keeping company." No need for it to be a secret.

"I thought that was him, but hoped otherwise."

Won't you tell me how long you were married, she longed to ask. Instead Lottie blurted out, "It's been sometime now, surely you've forgiven him," but she had no idea whatever for, hoping the woman would fill in what it was she needed to know.

Rhea let out a little gasp, as if she had received a blow. Lottie held out a hand to steady her, but was waved away. After a moment, she regained her composure. "You said you were making plans. You seem like a nice enough woman." Rhea's voice softened. She gave Lottie a look less of curiosity than concern, began to say more, then thought better of it.

"Maybe you can tell me, do they have dancing here? Sometimes in the evenings? Or on weekends?"

She gestured towards the Café, and pushed at the door. The temperature on the sidewalk changed, the air warmed by the smells of coffee and baking. And the sounds... spoons clinking softly against cups, talk proceeding as animated counterpoint. If you listened intently, you might even hear the intimate conversing of knees beneath white starched tablecloths.

"I've just recently discovered this delightful place. A bit reminiscent of those at home, don't you think?"

"Dancing? No, there's no dancing. If you don't mind, another personal question... Lottie hurried on before Rhea could disappear. She would grasp her arm if need be. Hold her there until she got her answer. "If you could do it over again, would you marry him?"

"Not on your life," Rhea snapped, without hesitation, making a rush for the door. It closed, and Lottie remained on the sidewalk, exiled.

Her fiancé would be here soon. Crossing the street, she walked until sure she was out of view of the Continental's patrons, but where she might still intercept Rudy. Of course they couldn't go back inside; Rhea had compromised their presence at the Café once and for all. Lottie didn't trust him to see her. The woman was bitter; there was no telling what she might do or say.

Rudy would find them another place, one which didn't allow cigars, where the waiters were not so familiar. But as for the Bee Cake, she would have to forego that pleasure. Pity. Specialty of the house and sure to be found nowhere else.

4

Lottie,

Forgive me. I know you would prefer any communication between us to be in English, but I need to muster what scant eloquence I possess to explain myself.

It has occurred to me you harbor some expectations of our relationship, and of myself, that I would be remiss not to correct. And, because events seem to be moving faster than you or I could have predicted, we must decide whether we should part company or continue on together.

Here you would cut me short. You believe nothing adverse will happen to you, and by extension, to us. But already, it may be too late. It is entirely my doing. I have not attempted with any enthusiasm to disillusion you.

Let me try now. I have a dubious future. It has been my sad experience this fact is the hardest for a woman to accept. I am a man uncomfortable in his adopted country. I am not good with my hands as your future brother-in-law would be quick to point out. You think my silence the result of deep rumination. You credit me with more intelligence simply because I have had more schooling. You would be surprised to find out how threadbare that intellectual coat is, dear Katz.

I believe your decision to return to the Café the following week at the same day and time insured our second encounter. And so here we are. But that we have come so far is largely my fault. I was through with women in any real sense when we met. Their responses were predictable, the outcome a foregone conclusion. But I never made this clear, teasing, pointing out one attractive female after another. This was meant to keep you at a distance. It only succeeded in making you more determined. I don't think you will let up now that you know about Rhea. You will never have any peace until you are sure you have replaced her in my heart. And of this, you will require proof.

Perhaps it is of some reassurance, and a wonder to me, after my first disastrous attempt at marriage, that I can even contemplate our life together. Why did I marry Rhea in the first place, you might ask. You saw for yourself; she is not unattractive. She held me in the correct measure of esteem, at least in the beginning. But she could make no allowances for my view of things. In fact, she took as a personal affront her inability to change my mind, or my habits. That especially rankled. Her anger was in direct proportion to her thwarted expectations. When I showed no move to provide her with the house and family she desired, she threatened to leave. The more I acknowledged this as a sad, but inevitable outcome of our union, the more she hung on. Perverse woman. For me, the major issues of my life had already been settled, but Rhea was young.

Oddly, she depended too much on my good opinion of her. I see, Lottie, how you disregard the judgements of others and make your own luck. Enough for both of us, I hope. Already my luck has changed, having found you. And I will not make a beggar of you; I can only do that to myself. You are safe from me in ways Rhea was not. It is my own safety that is in question.

I know you have ambition enough for the both of us. I have been warned. Your own sister said, "God help Lottie if she ever has to climb down off her high horse." My own wants are simpler. Long ago I gave up my taste for luxury since I had no practical means to satisfy it. You seem to manage in spite of the obstacles. You bring me presents, thinking you need to buy my affection. Or do the elegant shirt and silk tie make me more desirable in your eyes?

Do you notice when we walk--not as you prefer, with your arm linked through mine, but with my hand resting on the back of your neck--that you begin to carry both our weights, squaring your shoulders under the additional burden? Good little soldier. And so, my dear, we are going off to war. Or our version of it.

I asked you to join me at the camp, not to marry, because I did not wish to make that mistake twice. Being no fool, you, of course, could not agree to those terms. So I acquiesced. We will trade favors back and forth until I am the most heavily indebted.

I do not consider myself a man of promises. (It also annoyed Rhea that I could not show remorse over this.) But I do promise to keep from you this crack or fault in my nature, this weakness of the structure if you will, to hold it intact for however long it takes to cement our loyalty to one another. I have seen that loyalty in regard to your sister and brother. I am jealous now that I am outside of its embrace. But someday you will need those two. It will take a mighty transgression on my part, some compulsion stronger than what I feel for you. But sooner or later you will turn away from me. Perhaps, in time, you may even wish to do me physical harm.

You would run away first, to save yourself. (You may find that hard to believe now when we cannot get enough of one another, when we are both looking forward to being inside each other's skins.) I will not come after you. And when you return out of loyalty or remembrance of better times (but never out of pity), I will remind you that this marriage was all your idea.

Oh yes, I do care for you, the limits of which you seem to understand. I love your curious, spirited, optimistic nature, your fondness for the sound of your own voice. It's that same vanity that will convince you, in the face of mounting evidence to the contrary, of the wisdom of having chosen me as your husband. But what if I were to see that fine flattering light in which I now bask dimmed by a harsher assessment? Would I continue to hold you in the same regard? Do not ask that question. I am not sure I could, in truth, answer, "Yes."

Dare I mail this?

With all my affection,
Rudy

5

They picked their way among the ruins of the garden, stepping over the fractured paving and upturned rose bushes. A sewer line lay exposed in the open trench. The stone walls Gus had built to keep out the neighborhood children were showing signs of stress; one pillar had sloughed off its capital onto the sidewalk. Now several boys leaned against the walls, resting from their labors; they had been weaving a fort out of sumac branches in the vacant lot next door.

At the front door, Sabine gestured helplessly. "I wish the timing had been better."

Two reinforcing beams were wedged against the side of the house to keep it from settling any further. The braces seemed to be propping up the entire row of attached brick dwellings, which had been built on the clay of a casually drained swamp.

"If one goes, they all go," Rudy whispered, "Just like that." He snapped his fingers.

Inside, Sabine's artful prunings and salvaged roses were arranged in cut glass vases on the piano and sills. Gus had assembled the spiky aggressive house plants in a metal stand under the living room windows.

"The perfect background," Sabine said. She had held back a few flowers for Rudy's lapel and a bouquet rested on top of the beer and wine bottles in the refrigerator where the men now congregated around its open door. Sabine shoved Lottie up the stairs, noticing the scraped fabric on the heel of her sister's left shoe.

After days spent shopping for her wedding dress, Lottie was less than satisfied with her choice; there hadn't been time to make another. The shoes had been dyed to match, however, and Sabine had sewn a bit of tulle to one of her own hats.

Lottie changed in her sister's bedroom under the portrait of a younger self painted by an old boyfriend conspicuous in his absence. That melancholy person--hair severely drawn to the nape of her neck--was not the girlish woman smiling back in the glass, hair shorn in anticipation of new adventure. Searching in the drawer for a lace handkerchief, Lottie found a cache of bills Sabine kept for emergencies along with a box of chocolates, and was glad her sister was looking out for herself.

Downstairs, the guests, mostly Gus' relatives, sat precariously in chairs on the sloping wooden floor. The brothers-in-law were silent, wishing they were elsewhere. Maybe later, after the food and drinks were served, they would enter more energetically into the spirit of the proceedings. Now they listened to their wives praise the imaginative way their brother had transformed the living room, mirrors seeming to double the space; there was no escape from the lineup of solemn witnesses confronting their own truancy. Gus had finished repainting just hours before the ceremony. The smell of fresh labor reminded them of other walls waiting to be spackled, plastered or papered.

Sabine came down the stairs first. She was crying. Lottie followed, carrying her bouquet, the stems of the garden roses laced together with ribbon, their heads cuffed by a paper doily. Hans gave Lottie away. That left Gus to bang out the wedding march on the piano, his cigar burning in the glass ashtray next to the metronome.

The officiant waited in front of the plant stand. He had been engaged by Hedwig's husband, who was assured that he held no strong religious views. The man had been advised to choose words that would take into account the diverse beliefs of both the bride and groom, with whom he had never spoken. It was unclear what denomination, if any, he represented. Not too many questions were asked on either side; Lottie didn't want to delve too deeply into the matter of Rudy's first appearance at the altar. "All I want to know is, will it be legal?" As it turned out, the man had received his calling, and his papers, in the mail, his vocation as bell captain at the Waldorf-Astoria an added assurance that he would possess the right clothes for the occasion.

Rudy looked especially handsome in his dark suit and silk tie, the shoes that resembled dancing slippers. Anyone could see, Lottie thought, as he stood tall beside her, what a splendid choice she had made. She wondered whether Rudy was comparing this ceremony to his first, but then reassured herself that he had always sworn he remembered little of it.

The bell captain began reading from his pamphlet: "Rudy and Lottie, have you come here freely and without reservation to give yourselves to each other in marriage?"

Rudy looked surprised that the matter was to be settled so efficiently. Lottie thought he was waiting for a last-minute reprieve, but he nodded his quick assent along with hers.

"Since it is your intention to enter into marriage, join your right hands." Lottie hung on tightly. "Rudy do you take Lottie to be your wife? Do you promise to be true to her in good times and in bad, in sickness and in health, to love her and honor her all the days of your life?"

She held her breath. Rudy, she knew, was uncomfortable

making promises. After a telltale rock back on his heels, he said, "I do," loud and clear, turning to face his interrogator. To whom, Lottie wondered, was he making his pledge? Her own consent was muffled, her words drowned out, she was sure, by the beating of her heart. Hans smiled encouragement.

"The rings, please." Rudy slipped the band with the diamonds Lottie had purchased onto her lacquer-tipped finger.

"Take this," he said, "as a sign of my love and fidelity."

"Let us ask God for his continued blessings upon this couple," and here the captain hesitated, as if anticipating objections to the introduction of religion into the proceedings. When none were forthcoming, he pronounced the couple man and wife. Sabine's sobbing became audible; Lottie slipped her the lace handkerchief.

As the brother and sisters stood hemmed in by the greenery, Sabine was convinced they were together for the last time. In a few months she would take her own vows, but with Hedwig at her elbow as matron of honor. Lottie needed no urging to kiss her groom. Outside, in the vacant lot, the children sent up a shout; they had found another cat to torment.

The witnesses, Hans and Sabine, signed the papers, and then Rudy, much to Lottie's relief. Sabine was finally free to give Gus a dirty look and he tapped out the cigar. They toasted the couple with May wine, strawberries suspended in the glasses. The brothers-in-law eagerly kissed the bride and the groom resigned himself to kissing their wives. Sabine hugged herself with happiness, grabbing her own shoulders the way she had done as a child whenever things turned out better than her woeful predictions led her to expect.

6

Rudy took pleasure in the warm steam rising from the bucket, the flip of the rag as it came off the end of the rubber squeegee blade, the finishing swipe of the flanneled elbow. The repetitive motions lulled his mind into inventiveness and subversion; the most splendid schemes of civil disobedience came to him and then were as quickly dismissed. Leave that to the others. At this very moment, Willy might be stoking a fire in a less populated area of the camp. Pierre was cooling his heels in isolation for a more vocal offense. No such actions for a man like Rudy with divided loyalties.

He climbed down from the ladder, disgusted; months might go by before he was allowed to attack the film on the inside of the mess windows. By that time, grime or birds would have obliterated the care he had taken outside. If they suspected you were enjoying your work too much... He smiled to himself. The authorities didn't know what a specialist in glass the chemist had become.

He angled the ladder through the shed door and put the bucket with his tools on the floor. A drop of condensation fell onto the back of his neck. The other end of the rude structure had been converted by Pierre into a greenhouse. The bitter smell of decayed vegetation better suited his mood, the vivid colors of the zinnias almost a reproach. The authorities looked the other way at Pierre's scheme to sell the flowers in town, having become addicted to the fresh vegetables he grew between their rows. The anarchist turned capitalist.

. . .

It had been sometime since their committee, the full contingent, had met formally. No one remembered how the original members came to fall in together. A randomness marked their political affiliations and friendships. No sooner did a group settle by accident into some semblance of agreement, then it was disbanded and alliances rearranged. Even the men's given names had been lost, any peculiarity of temperament or appearance distilled into a label so that each came to be known by his abbreviated history.

Fish, who had spent the early months of conscientious service in a salmon hatchery, was already present wearing the flight jacket he never took off, a red flag in that place. He sat on the edge of his chair ready to bolt. He preferred to be outdoors in terrain too treacherous for other humans, but it was suspicious to set yourself too far apart.

George--this was not his real name--sat in the corner reading the paper. The talk was that his visit with his wife had gone badly. At one time in his life he had been a sentimental person; the nostalgic smell of newly applied wax to the laundry room floor could make him weep. George had been in the camp the longest. The committee members steered the new arrivals away from his misanthropic gaze. It was important to get the men while they were still fresh, but how to snag recruits while at the same time keeping a low profile? Their group had adopted none of the rites of a fraternal order, no special clothing or handshake by which to distinguish their eccentricities from the others.

"Cook." Rudy bowed to the stirrer of pots and gossip. Hansen greeted him with a cuff on the cheek.

"Kraut," he said, not without affection.

The two men set about dragging the tables into a "U" shape. The floor was marred from past meetings, chairs pushed away in anger, impatience, or simply boredom. Rudy checked the one on which he would be sitting at the head of the table for a broken crossbrace.

As secretary, it was Cook's job to do the setup. He cleared off the piles of linen. Bleached shirts and khaki pants were draped on the mangles; this was a place where what was once women's work was being done by, and for, men. The room where the laundry was folded, all of the rooms, lacked domestic comforts, no pillows or upholstered furniture. "They don't want any part of us to get soft," Fish had said. No pictures adorned the walls. Personal items were better kept close at hand; compact, like the men's nicknames, small enough to be carried away at a moment's notice.

Clocks, with their intricate, almost feminine cases, a holdover from another, less rigid order, were spaced evenly about the walls for maximum effect, a reminder of what a man might create given encouragement and the right materials. Bender, the first camp president, had kept them in perfect working order, but since his departure, each face displayed an independent and willfully inaccurate version of the time as it was proceeding in London, Paris, Berlin, Tokyo. Accuracy was of little concern except when the men ventured out on furlough. Of Colorado Mountain Time there was no reference. The camp bells tolled those hours, calling them to their beds, to meals, to work.

The installation of the clocks and Bender's presidency had coincided with the inception of regular meetings, the administration's attempt to impress some visiting congressman that the democratic process was still alive at the camp. This was before monotonous chores dulled the collective civic spirit. The system fell apart almost from the beginning. It was easy enough to choose a representative from each barracks, which took on the coloration of its most vocal members, but less simple to find a spokesman for the entire diverse camp population which was made up of Social and Christian Democrats, atheists, religious fanatics, not to mention the occasional saboteur.

Older than the rest, Bender had been more like a disapproving parent. In matters of integrity, he was unmoveable. At any mention of a slowdown or demonstration, he became nervous; his religious beliefs would not allow him to condone such activities. He felt a moral obligation to try to dissuade the men from any disruptive action. When it became apparent to the administration that Bender's meticulousness extended beyond timepieces to matters of conscience, that he was respected by most factions, they began to cast about for another camp to place him, where the inmates were less impressionable. After his wife left and he began wetting the bed, Bender refused to get up in the mornings, clinging to the damp sheets. There was a widely held opinion that the stupidest thing the authorities did was to allow Bender to transfer out, making room for that atheist and troublemaker, Pierre. Let Bender be a lesson to us all, Rudy thought.

It was, in actuality, Pierre's turn to chair the meeting. They rotated the position, diluting the sense of power. Like the bastard tennis they played using racquets with broken strings, the one who served had the advantage. You could make up the rules as you went along.

Pierre was absent. Rudy was next in line. To prepare himself, he had been practicing his oratory skills in front of the shaving mirror. This time he believed he would be able to coax the men out of their torpor, to raise them to an enthusiastic pitch, bending their collective wills around the idea of action, whatever that might be. In his imagination he heard loud and prolonged clapping. The next moment he would bring them down, accompanied by vigorous foot stamping, in vehement denunciation against some administrative folly. Never in his life would he have the opportunity to move men so. It would be a little, he thought, like conducting an orchestra.

"Looks like just us," Rudy said. "We might as well proceed."

Cook had washed glasses, set out ashtrays and a bottle of whiskey in the center of the table. He put out no paper or pencils, convinced it was better that nothing be written down. He was proud of his memory. Still, too much time was spent setting the record straight or, depending on how one looked at it, clouding the issues further. Cook had no talent whatsoever for keeping a secret. Badgered, sometimes threatened when something said in confidence was repeated and then traced back to him, he offered up his resignation at least once a month, but no one stepped forward to take his place. This position, like his other as purveyor of their meals, was won, and maintained, by default. From a brown paper bag he now extracted three carrots, the dirt still clinging to the roots.

"Where's the agenda?" Rudy asked, hopeful. The agenda was never posted or distributed. It seldom mattered. The items were always the same: access to midnight snacks, personal cars, movies. Women.

"There are important matters to discuss." Pierre stood in the doorway, leaning against the frame, less for drama than support. A small man in the healthiest of times, he seemed to have shrunk since they last saw him. His face betrayed the ravages of a childhood illness he had contracted the year before undergoing vaccination testing. Cook rushed forward to embrace him.

"Easy, you'll kill me," Pierre said.

"You've lost a bit of weight, I can see that. It's your convictions that will finally do you in, my friend." Cook looked down. "But I admire your taste in footwear." Pierre struck a dancer's pose, extending one leg for all to see. A strict vegetarian, he refused to wear shoes made of leather, even while in the hospital undergoing treatment for infection. Thrown into isolation, he meditated over the peeling soles of his feet. In a show of support for his release, some of the men also decided to go barefooted, but after a few days cutting brush, this proved to be impractical. It was Cook who came up with the suggestion of issuing Pierre canvas shoes, in one brilliant stroke saving both Pierre's feet and his principles.

"Here, new guidelines to be committed to memory." From inside his shoe Pierre extracted a crumpled sheet of paper. Last week he had sent word they were to refuse to participate in target practice.

Cook sighed audibly, like a man whose favorite toy was about to be taken from him. He read aloud: "Don't pick sugar beets, used in the manufacture of glycerine. Don't work on flax." He looked up, confused.

Pierre explained, "The linseed oil is used to make explosives."

Cook was relieved. The first two would be easy; flax or

sugar beets didn't grow at that elevation. But the last item
gave him pause: "No more plane spotting." He had few pleasures, chief of which was to climb the fire tower ladder, sit
crosslegged on the hatch cover and aim his binoculars at the
sky and nearby trees. With his field guide close at hand, he
kept a running tally of the birds he observed. If an incidental
plane crossed his field of vision, what harm would it do to call
it in? This was a game where there were no others, matching
the silhouettes of the planes with those on the wall chart, the
birds with those pictured in the book.

"Also," Pierre added, "guard duty is out. We have to be
together on this, understood?" It was unlikely Cook, or any
of the others, would ignore Pierre's wishes. They all looked to
him to see how far they dare go, but any retaliatory impulses
were usually tempered by Pierre's more practical motives.

Cook had his own agenda, which included sitting out the
war with a minimum of inconvenience, doing as little as possible until hostilities were over. This went against a natural incli-
nation he had to meddle and gossip but it was not in his best
interest for the little anarchist to push too hard, to attract too
much attention to their group. Cook breathed easy only when
he could keep Pierre, who had been a botanist in his other life,
confined to the greenhouse, agitating over his vegetables.

"Who's taking over as the master of ceremonies this
evening," Pierre asked. "You, Kraut?"

"Which of us Krauts do you mean? The German American
or the echt German?" Willy had entered unobserved. "I'm
more German than this guy." He slipped an arm over Rudy's
shoulder.

"A matter of opinion," Rudy said, disentangling himself
and taking the chair at the end of the table closest to the exit,

but not without complaint. "Slivers." He kicked at the furniture in disgust, having given up all hope of presiding over the meeting.

"Let me see," Willy said. He grabbed Rudy's hand and kissed the palm.

It was hard to dislike Willy. Even though for years the man's ancestors had been traveling back and forth across the border from the Sudatenland, practicing a dual citizenship, he considered himself first and foremost, a German. Not like all those itinerant Dutchmen, Rudy thought, who would revert back to being midwestern Catholics after the war.

"You like me," Willy had said shortly after they met, settling the matter. He was never less than straight forward, in such a place, not a wise thing. Rudy knew the authorities considered Willy too dangerous for the trenches. When they wouldn't place him in the munitions factory in a town near his wife's relatives, she divorced him.

Willy punched Pierre in the arm. "See who's come back to haunt us. The ghost of our departed consciences."

"Have a little respect." Pierre sat at the head of the table, poured himself a shot from the bottle and squinted at the glass before taking a sip.

"To get out," he said, "I had to promise not to drink and to avoid all association with persons of bad reputation." He gestured towards Willy, then downed the rest, refusing to relinquish his hold on the liquor, which was against all the rules. "Can we have the report on the greenhouse first? Willy, how many of my seedlings did you trample under your big, German boot?"

"Gentlemen," Rudy reminded them, "This meeting has yet to be called to order."

"Here," said Cook, holding up the carrots, "here is the evidence."

"What do you suppose the spaces between the rows are for, Willy?" Pierre asked. It squared with Willy's conscience to involve himself in the production of the food that went to feed the men in camp, but it was work he was ill suited for.

They learned the nature of Willy's specialty when he was discovered trying to ignite some rags in a barrel near the dump. He was delighted with himself, his charred eyebrows a badge of honor. "I had you guessing for awhile," he said. He was a master at setting fires which had a high nuisance value. Detected before they became serious, they peppered the camp, causing flares of excitement like Cook's grease fires, extinguished as quickly as started.

The men looked at Willy in a new light, the way they looked at anyone who could temper his passions in the service of a higher cause. It was understood that the man who provided the most diversions was the next in line as leader in case a transfer should occur.

"Willy's too busy daydreaming to mind where he walks. La, la, Willy is in love," Cook teased.

"That's none of our business," Rudy said. "And it has nothing to do with why we're here tonight. Pierre, put down the bottle. Talk now, drinks later."

"All I know is that she was a patient in the hospital where Willy played nurse for awhile," Cook continued. "And that she wants him to enlist, something to do with tapping into the aid-to-dependents fund."

The color rose in Willy's face. "Can I help it if these healing hands..."

"I've seen her. She has thighs like Pierre's turnips," Cook said. Even Willy had to laugh at this.

"Shut up you two. You're both out of order. Minutes from the last meeting, please." Rudy had taken hold of the gavel.

Cook stood and delivered a string of excuses. That old one, "You spoke too quickly."

"All of us?" Rudy asked, skeptical.

George furiously waved his hand, then broke in, not waiting to be recognized. "What's to remember? The same things. Always the same."

"Ah-h-h. George is right. We go around and around and get nowhere," Fish said, talking through his nose. He had been baling hay. He was riddled with allergies. He dabbed at his eyes with a grey handkerchief. "I have no sense of smell anymore," he lamented.

"What about the Treasurer's Report?" George asked. He kept a box under his bed ready to secure any funds that they might entrust to him. There never were any. What little money they had they cajoled from their wives, although they all did what they could to earn a few dollars. Fish killed snakes and sold the skins. Their pay from camp work was impounded and placed in a fund frozen in a bank in Washington, D.C.; the courts had yet to decide who had legal access. "We'll never see any of it," George said.

The other men were more optimistic. They had decided that their communal portion of the money, if it was forthcoming, should be used for a soccer team because that would include their greatest number. Willy was pushing for it because he was small and at a disadvantage in other team sports. Cook wanted to be goalie. Only George had to be persuaded the project had merit.

Groups from the other barracks had their own ideas about how the money should be spent. The academics in "C" were urging that guest lecturers be invited.

Pierre scoffed. "Do you know what they'd allow? Talks on flower arranging. Or worse, throw in some administrative propaganda. They can't take a chance any of us might get close to an intelligent idea."

Pierre was secretly hoping he would be asked to speak on plant genetics, but knew even those men who had been teachers weren't allowed to address the camp formally; who knew what disruptive philosophies they might introduce. Informally, among themselves, the men were their own best censors, never able to agree on a topic for discussion.

Each barracks put up posters, advertising its dream project. These papered the camp, even the latrine. Each night they were removed or plastered over by proponents with other interests; each day they were tacked up anew.

Lottie was secretly rooting for the group that wanted to purchase instruments and form a band; they might need a singer. The choral group protested when they got wind of the idea; they thought their request for sheet music more realistic, considering the amount of money they were likely to receive. "Those guys don't think big enough," George said.

The other wives made their wishes known. Cook's wife, who had decided to go into the butchering business, had already priced a set of knives. When he had enough to drink, Cook complained about how demanding she was getting lately;

sober, he never mentioned it.

"Can we skip over the Treasurer's Report and get to the heart of things?" Pierre asked. "The greenhouse report." He looked hard at Willy.

"Just for once," Rudy asked, "could we discuss something other than lettuce?" There was mumbled agreement.

Pierre was indignant. "Ingrates." After all, he thought, they were all delighted whenever fresh vegetables appeared on their plates. Left to himself, with no thought of improving their social consciences or suppers, Pierre would be content to grow his plants and gather his seeds.

Kristen, his wife, sold Pierre's flowers in town, wrapping them in damp newspaper for the bus trip, refusing to accompany Lottie, who had the only car. "Letting her drive, you know, you're asking for trouble," Pierre said. The other women preferred to thumb rides out to the camp, believing a car belonged rightfully to the husband. The husbands didn't want their wives to be able to pick up and leave whenever they had a mind to, although with gas rationing they wouldn't get far.

"Cook, you were going to look into the possibility of getting late-night snacks." Rudy raised his voice.

"Why bother?" asked George. "There's never anything decent to eat."

"How about fruit? I've seen it, lying on the road, waiting to be picked up. Apples, pears, ground under the wheels of cars and trucks. A waste."

Rudy knew that his wife wasn't too proud to pick up the fallen apples. Encouraged by some of those who had tasted her fruit cakes, Lottie had tried unsuccessfully to sign on as the camp baker, but supporting the dependent of a C.O. was against all the rules.

"You're a fool, Cook, to talk about waste in this place. And as for that fruit," George said, "you can gather it at risk to your own hide."

Their presence in town was barely tolerated. As conditions worsened overseas, the incidences of name calling, shoving, and out-and-out brawling had increased. But the men kept silent in camp about the war, as if they had no right to discuss it; they would sooner talk about what went on with their wives in the Common Room. But that didn't mean that the subject wasn't uppermost in their minds.

Willy said, exasperated, "What do we do? Make dirt and clean it up again, dig holes and fill them in." He thought it was time for another demonstration, perhaps another fire.

"Nothing so drastic," Pierre cautioned. "A slowdown. Maybe."

"Maybe," Willy said, "that last stretch in isolation has turned you soft."

"Did you hear about Cutler's latest stunt?" Admiration was in Fish's voice. "Spent two days building a fence that wouldn't keep anything out. When he was reprimanded, that wiseacre told them, 'You didn't say you wanted me to string wire, only that I was to put the staples into the posts.'"

This was a man who erected a partition around his bed for privacy; Cutler found occasion for challenge in the simplest aspects of existence. When the partition came down, so did the curtains in all the barracks.

"I guess the rest of us can count on our furloughs being cancelled, or, at best, postponed; they can use the excuse it's getting into fire season, or just announce a blanket suspension 'for administrative reasons,'" Rudy said.

"People like Cutler just bring down a lot of trouble on

themselves, not to mention others." Cook was nervous. He didn't like the direction in which the discussion was heading; already he was mentally erasing it. He was happy enough, however, to pass on the rumor that someone was about to be transferred to Germfask, the camp where a bunch of dirty, unshaven men weren't even required to make their own beds. For Cook, this purposeless existence seemed like paradise.

"Naw. Won't be Cutler," Fish said. "Cutler's smart. He's made himself indispensable."

"That's a laugh," Pierre said, bitterly.

Personally, Rudy thought Fish was right. They all knew about the black list. Cutler wasn't on it or he would have been transferred long ago. But its existence was confirmed every time one of their requests to be assigned to more desirable work was summarily dismissed. A man could become para-noid. How else explain why he was saddled with kitchen duty in the balmiest of weather and turned outside for road work the minute the sky darkened.

Rudy was sure his name was on that list. He had put in for transfer to a relief training camp where they studied languages, first aid, the social conditions of devastated areas. He figured he was a natural, speaking the language as he did, an expert on the culture.

"Forget about it," Willy said, "that would make too much sense." Instead they offered him training in cooking, truck driving, carpentry. He then asked to be transferred to Mancos. At least there the Director showed some interest in matching up a man's work with his abilities.

At Mancos, the men got a dollar a month to purchase athletic equipment or books. There were curtains on the windows, even the occasional windowbox; all reported in the

Mancos paper until it folded when the editor was transferred to Germfask after writing a seditious piece on the high divorce rate among C.O.'s.

As an exercise, Rudy had begun translating the papers into German, then tackled some magazine articles, but Willy had deemed his versions "a bit dry." Rudy couldn't dispute this, playing it safe, transposing word for word, the diligent, precise schoolboy.

"The trouble is," Willy had said, "you're unfamiliar with the context in which the piece was written. You're missing the flavor entirely. Not your specialty. Better stick to windows."

Rudy didn't know why he had thought this evening would be any different. "Enough news about the old gang," he said.

The meetings all followed a pattern: complaints, gossip. If they did discuss something of value, he noticed it was the man who spoke loudest and ran off at the mouth who was least informed. And when it came time to vote, none were persuaded by the rhetoric, their ballots predetermined long before all discussion began. Most meetings deteriorated into whining sessions over the facilities, unkempt lockers and muddy floors, or attacks against those who wouldn't take part in the general housekeeping.

"It's not as if picking clothes up off the floor involved you in the administration of conscription," Cook said.

This was a sheepish lot, Rudy thought; the goats had all been driven to another camp before they could insinuate themselves into the flock.

"A new crop of scrubs is due anyday." Pierre made this announcement in the nature of "Other Business," a catch-all phrase that enabled them to drift even further from the nonexistent agenda. "Any ideas?"

"Give it up," George said. "That's a lost cause." The Director had a good nose for sniffing out the best men before the group had a crack at them. To these he gave "the treatment," a private talk, maybe over a private lunch. Soon they would comprehend and then resign themselves to the lack of design or rationale in the work assignments.

Cutler, who boasted he had some German in his background, instructed the town bootmaker to put metal taps on the heels of his shoes which he insisted on clicking in time to the singing of the national anthem. The group carefully watched the reaction of the new arrivals, noting who displayed the most dedicated demeanor towards the music, who the most shock at Cutler's irreverence; these they quickly ruled out. It was that nondescript middle ground they were looking for.

Rudy advised them to, "Concentrate on the 4-F's." He had thought he would be passed up because of his own ingrown toenails.

"Don't worry," the Army reassured him, "we'll have you into a pair of boots in no time."

When they fixed Rudy's feet, and having no religious affiliation that mandated his conscientious objection to the war, he fell back on his citizenship. He refused to apply for naturalization papers. Rudy had objected to the question on the form about whether the applicant intended to bear arms for the United States in future wars; he managed to convince them that carrying a weapon wasn't the issue, just the direction in which it would be pointed.

"We don't want any grousers," George said. Grousers, they all knew, turned into troublemakers, eventually into saboteurs. "Okay, here's what we got. A 4-Fer, who's quiet, like Rudy here. The model recruit." Rudy smiled, showed them some teeth. He had never thought of himself as a model of anything before. He decided he liked these guys after all. "About the only thing wrong with Rudy is, he's a Kraut."

There was a bad feeling among the men in general about the way the German POW's were treated at other camps. Better in some ways, even than the inmates at Mancos. They were allowed to receive packages: liquor, chocolate, cigarettes. If that was so, Rudy didn't begrudge them this, knowing something about being deprived of family and country.

Two bells rang out in short succession followed by two more.

"Oh, what now?" They should ignore the interruption and go on, Rudy thought. It would be such a small act of defiance, not to appear in the yard when one was expected. Again two bells and then silence. George squirmed uncomfortably. Fish shoved back his chair; he could go either way. Pierre was aware the men were waiting to see if he would rise. He rubbed a carrot against his shirt and took a bite, thinking it over.

"Is it a fire? Who's on watch?" George asked. This could make all the difference.

Pierre lept to his feet. "Be grateful for the break in the monotony. We were getting nowhere. Nothing is being accomplished here."

Cook looked relieved. "Two bells. Just a fire drill, I think," he said, trying to downplay his working knowledge of the camp rules.

"Can we be sure this isn't the real thing?" George looked suspiciously at Willy, who only shrugged his shoulders.

They vacated the laundry room, counting off to the smack of Pierre's shoes on the floor, hard march on "left," one by one falling in behind, the cadence slightly off.

Rudy remembered the photograph of his father in a dark uniform and pointed cap, the braid a white loop across his chest; as a child he had believed meritorious Army service had earned him those pieces of ribbon. The decorations, he later found out, were traditional on a miner's dress uniform, worn for a formal portrait the day of the union parade. Rudy got over his disappointment, which was replaced by an overwhelming desire to leave home.

"Are you ever afraid, having to work underground all the time?" he once asked his father; Rudy could think of nothing the man had done that could possibly merit such punishment.

"It's not so bad, really. In time, you can get used to anything," the answer meant to be reassuring, but in its way more frightening than the prospect of descending into the earth each day.

Pierre stuck his head back in the door, "Remember the whiskey," he admonished. Little chance of that, Rudy thought, flourishing the bottle and bringing up the rear.

7

Lottie eased off her shoes, but resisted the temptation to put her feet up on the cot. Rudy mustn't see her lying down. There was much to talk over first. Once she had fallen asleep waiting. While she slept, he had tucked her tightly into the sheets.

On the opposite wall a target held two darts tossed far from the mark. A bouquet of bent stems, Pierre's flowers, were wedged into a canning jar. The water needed changing.

The cot was placed so that it faced a window with an unobstructed view of a tree, the tallest among the giants in the distance. It had been ravaged by lightning, the tip a charred spike. Rudy imagined scaling its limbs one day, climbing as high as possible into thinner, clearer air. He told Lottie that the view, over all the roofs of the camp buildings, would out-weigh any risk.

From her string bag she took a plastic radio. She crawled under the cot to plug in the cord. There were remnants of other trysts and she came up with a sorry look on her face, wiping the dust from her hands and knees. The candle placed on the chair that served as an end table, the flowers, the radio, these items were meant to counter the effects of the dart board and utilitarian cot. But papers and bottles overflowed from trash cans in the hall. Overhead, the spiders went about their work undisturbed. After the wives complained, threatening never to set foot in the Common Room again, a half-hearted attempt was made to sweep up; the men went so far as to hang curtains. A couch appeared, one damask cushion missing, its springs poised to skewer the unwary. The cot was strictly for romantic encounters, which occurred every two weeks, the authorities decreeing this to be a good average, while the couch became the prickly site of more businesslike discussions. As soon as this sad amenity was taken for granted, it disappeared, along with the curtains.

On their anniversary, Rudy arranged for his wife to stay overnight. He accomplished this only after careful plotting and with the complicity of all the men in the barracks. The next morning, rather than face an embarrassed silence, Lottie slipped away before breakfast. Such visits were meant to encourage morale. More often than not, they had the opposite effect, reminding the men of what they were missing. The husbands were concerned about being forgotten, or replaced by more practiced lovers.

"Who's left out there?" Lottie was reassuring. "Just old men, defectives, school boys."

Conjugal visits were often scheduled for the weekends back to back, the number of women on the only bus returning to town on Saturday evenings evidence of perfunctory and hurried encounters.

"Oh, we never completely undress," Kristen confessed to Lottie. "I think at any minute our time will be up. I don't dream about anything except being next to him, our purely naked bodies touching for an entire afternoon." She spread her fingers and hid her face behind them.

No one wanted to be penciled in last, to miss the bus, forced to hitch a ride at dusk when it was hard to see the face of the person who stopped. Impossible, in that dim light, to judge how angry the driver was with anyone who had been visiting the camp.

One Sunday morning, while the residents and personnel were occupied with church services, Kristen and Pierre had conspired to meet, but spent their precious hour turning away a series of individuals eager to make converts. Kristen scarcely had time to slip out of her dress.

Lottie was sympathetic but the friendship between the women didn't extend much beyond a common interest in supporting themselves. For the most part, Lottie saved what she earned from mending broken zippers in uniforms; she considered the change she sometimes found in the pockets a bonus. But she was an easy mark for any cream that boasted of startling transformations in her appearance. The bathroom shelves were full of such promises, and she couldn't bring herself to throw these out even after they proved disappointing.

She lavished equal attention on her hands. Her wedding ring boasted one large and three smaller diamonds at a time when most women were satisfied with a plain band. A gift to herself, she had purchased it before they left for camp so everyone would see in what good opinion she was held by her spouse.

Every so often she bought something for Sabine. Her sister would praise the gifts in her letters, but Lottie knew she put them away in the boxes they had come in. A ceramic bird she kept for herself. A pet of sorts, since her landlady wouldn't allow even the company of a parakeet. "No pets, no children," she said, checking for telltale signs whenever her tenant was away at the camp. Lottie felt it was unlikely that she and Rudy would ever be able to afford children. Sabine, the youngest, was already expecting a baby. But someday, Lottie thought, she and Rudy would have a house. And there would be noone to say she couldn't have a yard full of chickens if that was what she wanted.

Lottie sat on the edge of the cot in her slip, a ledger open on her lap. It was important to put something down, anything, no matter how insignificant the amount; the accounting was almost as important as the bills and coins themselves. The pages were a reckoning of what she had been doing: earning a living. She had done that before, on the farm, and in the employment of Mrs. Stevens, but always with a sense that the situation she found herself in was a temporary one. She seemed now to be occupying her future.

The sums became decidedly smaller. Most men were anticipating getting out of their camp clothes soon and didn't need, or want, any mending done. Lottie had become less optimistic. "You'll never be let out of here," she told Rudy, "not until every last soldier has come home."

The entries made quickly, she drew two lines across the bottom of the page. Once she had awaited her husband's arrival with eagerness. Now the suspense was unnerving; she was uncertain as to what disposition she would find him in today, uncertain as to whether she could muster the correct response. Believing that love would be the most important factor in her life, she had followed its dictates. She looked around the room, their bedchamber. The cost was proving too dear. She wouldn't let herself dwell on this. There were days when Lottie was convinced Rudy could do anything. When told he needed glasses, he began a series of rigorous eye exercises so that, in time, he could pick out a smoke spiral on a nearby mountain, or add a rare specimen to Cook's tally of birds.

Usually Rudy arrived first; he would meet Lottie at the door, closing it gently behind them and, his arm around her waist, guide her to the cot. More and more he had been withdrawing into himself, cooperating less and less in their intimacy. When the men hatched a particularly brash scheme, he refused to participate, acting disinterested; when the scheme backfired, his silence became a damning "I told you so." That was fine with Lottie. She didn't want him making any trouble, didn't want him transferred to another camp. If they were forced to move, what would happen to her plans?

She couldn't appeal to his conscience; that was what had put him here in the first place. Sometimes, while making love, he would whisper endearments in German, and she would put a correcting finger to his lips. She urged him to use English, even when they were alone. She had left all of that behind, willingly, years before. In truth, it had been in steps, not like Rudy, who took one reckless leap and kept looking back. From the time her parents had put her on the train to East Prussia, Lottie had been headed on this course. East, West, the direction was all the same. Away from home.

When Rudy came in, she rose to meet him. On his hands she saw the ink of wet newsprint, sniffed the telltale odor of kerosene which he had come by illegally. He smelled of his work. His feet were bare. His shoes, he explained, had been stolen.

"The boys are having a little fun with me," he said, proudly.

"I should get you some slippers."

Always she brought something; always he expected a

present. Once, money had been tighter than usual and she had arrived emptyhanded.

"What's the matter," he said testily, "aren't you shaking the pockets hard enough?"

Lottie left abruptly that day, grateful, once again, that she had her own transportation. It was then she started keeping secrets from him, although at first they had only to do with money.

Rudy never said he was sorry, but would softly call her "Cat," a name he had given her at the beginning of their courtship because of the whipped cream she heaped into her coffee. It was meant to remind her of their Café days, of the anticipation of seeing him there, his head bent over a newspaper. Who was that attractive fellow? And then the sweet realization it was for her he waited.

Lottie's mouth felt dull, her tongue coated, as if she needed to brush her teeth. She wished she could open the bottle now, rather than later.

Rudy undressed slowly. Often they joked about how the pants removed hastily in that room meant more business for the seamstress. He watched his wife pull the slip over her head, feeling it impolite to stare, longing to speed up the process, but it was Lottie who touched him first, on the shoulder. She sat close enough now so that he could see her eyes. He touched her leg. She had recently shaved, clear up the thigh.

The last time they had gone to the beach, just before their departure for the camp, Lottie sat on the blanket, leaning back and supporting herself with her arms. She had taken off her skirt, because she owned no bathing suit, and pulled down the straps of her brassiere, but already there were white bands on the pale shoulders and he wondered about those other times she had gone to the beach without him. Rudy settled his head on Lottie's stomach and fell asleep. They had both paid for their lack of caution the next day, howling when their burnt skin was touched, but when Rudy thought he wouldn't be able to manage their short time together, he remembered that day at the beach, Lottie's white thighs flared out on the blanket above her delicate knees, and was able to begin.

"Wait." She turned on the radio. Music came on, then static. "Anything will do," Rudy said, impatient. She tried wriggling out of his grasp, reaching over to fool with the knob.

"Leave it, it doesn't matter." He pushed her down onto the bed, onto her back. Rudy got serious quickly; no matter how much she teased in an effort to slow him down, he went deeper, became more focused until he had reclaimed what the government had taken from him the last two weeks. She wished it was different, but understood. The second time, it was always better, slower, the intensity spaced with talk.

Lottie looked out the window over Rudy's shoulder and watched the lifting of the alder leaves, a hint of some coolness outside; it was so hot in here, she thought. Rudy was perspiring now. She longed to get up and bring a towel before they began again; surely he would want to. First, he would sit up and stare at the opposite wall, at the picture of the bearded Jesus someone had nailed there, at the ceiling, or out the window at his tree. Then, just as abruptly, he would resume, with renewed energy, or imagination; she hoped he had been thinking of her.

Rudy lay inside Lottie now, occasionally moving, sighing, beginning to fall asleep. She began to feel a sense of urgency. She had so many things to attend to, so many decisions that required they talk. It was time to expand the business. She was going to sell the car, their chief asset, to buy a newer sewing machine and materials. She had never shown any interest in making her own clothes but now, whenever she was attracted to a dress, she took it down from the hanger and inspected the seams to see how they were finished.

Before she could grab him, Rudy rolled over. Lottie wanted him to hold on a bit longer, to make amends for her inattention. Well, now she could admire him. Rudy's hair had been recently shorn, as if Pierre had gotten at him with the gardening shears. The tips of his ears were showing; he appeared pathetic, endearing. The face had seen too much of the sun lately, his mouth opening and closing around an imaginary circle, the rib cage rising and falling in its sheath of delineated muscle. Rudy had been working outside with the road crew, putting in 54-hour weeks, redoing a section of paving until the grade was pronounced, "just right." He didn't share her outrage; they might tire his body, but would never exhaust his capacity to outwit them. Outside, someone was whistling, competing with the static on the radio, a melody she had heard before, from "Der Rosenkavalier." Even in a place like this a person could find something to put his heart into. She began to hum, reaching over to switch off the radio, waking Rudy. He rubbed his stiff arm on which she had been lying and shook out a cigarette from the pack always within easy reach. She had given up the habit when it proved too expensive and found herself begrudging him this simple pleasure.

From the bottle on the chair he poured a shot of whiskey in one glass, and two in another. He took a sip of the fuller glass, and then a pull on the cigarette, his mind elsewhere. Lottie sensed this wasn't the time to mention the car. Was there something she might tell him, something she had been doing the last two weeks that didn't involve expense? How she had painted her room in the stucco bungalow to offset some of the rent, in her enthusiasm the paint dripping onto the few pieces of good furniture they owned, wedding presents from Hans and Sabine. Well, she would leave out that bit. A hand placed judiciously here or there, and Rudy wouldn't want to talk or to listen. "How easy," she thought, "how much too easy." But Lottie couldn't get the whistler's tune out of her head. She wasn't one to give in to nostalgia, believing it was dangerous to look backwards, but this time not even Rudy's ministrations could gather her distracted thoughts. Her eyes were drawn to the egg casings tucked into the corners of the ceiling. She imagined the sweep of a broom pulling at the sticky wrappings, closed her eyes against the slow, fluttering descent of the cottonlike wombs, and gave herself up to the present.

The last thing Rudy did before bidding Lottie goodbye was to give her the pants that needed mending. She wondered about what pointed and powerful objects were kept in the pockets to make so many holes. The more holes, the more money she made.

"It amounts to next to nothing," she told Rudy, but bought a few stocks on a wide margin. She told herself he would only laugh at her grand schemes. "The Depression wasn't so long ago, didn't she remember anything?" He would start sounding like Gus, her brother-in-law, whose unquestioning belief wasn't in the financial institutions themselves but in the solid masonry that housed them.

Rudy would expect a really good bottle of something

special if he smelled extra money. "That will come in good time," Lottie told herself and hugged him quickly, leaving before he could divine what his wife was thinking, that she carried their fortunes in her hands.

As the war accelerated into its final days, the men didn't dare seek relief in town; the local VFW groups patrolled the roads, erecting makeshift barriers of their vehicles and filling in the gaps with linked arms. When townspeople were hard pressed to visit ill relatives, or attend funerals because of the scarcity of gas, the sight of a truckload of men intent on getting drunk, was incendiary. The Common Room became the only distraction, that, and practical, often cruel, jokes. The more certain the outcome of the conflict, the more uncertain the mood of the committee members, who met seldom these days. They kept their thoughts from one another and slept badly. How would they act on the outside? More importantly, how would others react to them? Fish wondered if he would ever respond to his Christian name since this one suited him, he felt, so much better.

Rudy had refused to allow Lottie to sell the car. It was just as well, because when he was released, they were among the first able to get away. Lottie was looking forward to seeing her sister and new niece. Rudy had told his wife he would go wherever she wished, that he could practice his trade anyplace; he had gotten into the habit of having her make those decisions.

Cook's wife had begun fixing up a big unwieldy house in town; it had served as a funeral parlor until the undertaker was drafted. She had already written to her relatives to join them. Her husband would start a restaurant, although they all advised Cook that he made a better secretary. Fish found out he liked his creatures better alive than dead. He had taken to borrowing the field guide, pointing out to the other reluctant ornithologists on the road crew what they were missing. Willy signed on to work as a cattle attendant on a relief ship and Rudy took every opportunity to tease him about becoming a sea cowboy, envious that his friend was able to delay a bit longer the decision about what to do when he got out. George was jealous that Willy got to avoid the company of humans for awhile, including the woman patient who seemed to have healed herself and moved on. Kristen said all that was needed to restore the old, optimistic George was a job that would use his talents, but no one knew what those might be. As for her husband, Pierre planned to give up teaching and go into politics, after much deliberation hanging onto his French name tag rather than reverting back to the more Germanic, Max. They all, except Rudy, promised to vote for him; he said it was nothing personal.

Lottie and Rudy drove off, but not before honking and circling the greenhouse where Pierre was saying his own good-byes. Rudy made Lottie stop first at the cemetery so he could tip his hat to those men whose people had yet to claim them. Bender had gone home from another camp on a stretcher, but Cutler hadn't made it out because he hadn't wanted to. They set off to find their tree, but the distance to the lone spire proved too far and they turned back towards the highway.

"Is there enough gas?" Rudy asked.

"We'll make it enough," Lottie said, glad he had agreed they would live with her sister, but disheartened about how little he had struggled against it.

They settled in with Sabine and Gus, indebting Rudy to a man whose views he soon found intolerable. When Rudy tried to find work, he was asked where he had been during the war, had he "served time?" It sounded as if they were asking whether he had ever been in prison and the answer was "yes" on both counts. Still, there were days when he missed it.

Lottie had embraced American citizenship with the fervor she approached anything that enabled her to distance herself from the past; she assumed Rudy would follow her lead. Her husband balked at having to take an oath renouncing allegiance to all foreign powers and promising to support and defend the Constitution. He had lost all taste for authority, even in its abstract form, the citizenship of his heart remaining steadfast.

It was about this time that Lottie had an abortion. The two sisters managed it themselves without their customary neatness. The medical treatment available wasn't the best, particularly for someone with so telling an accent; Lottie, too, was on some list. Later she would swear to Sabine it was just as well, when Rudy was earnestly into his drinking, that no children ever came.

8

Once again Rudy found himself in a room designed for one purpose and distorted into another. Pleated fabric hid the base of the sink and the pots stored beneath it. From this spare bedroom transformed into their kitchen, he had a clear view through the vine maple, its branches denuded by gypsy moths, across the alley. In an identical window, a night light burned; someone else was having trouble sleeping.

Sipping a glass of water, imagining the occupant of that room propped against a brace of pillows, reading in his own bed, Rudy found no answer to the recurring question of how he had come to be in this place. The sense of the randomness of his life was overwhelming.

He had been careful not to wake his wife. Lottie would be lying on her back now, arms flung out to the side, having claimed the extra bed space, impossible to budge. Once he had only to touch her, even in sleep, and her body would coil naturally towards his own. Now, no amount of prodding or rearranging of her limbs could produce the desired movement.

She was a late riser. The men had already gone to work. Through the common wall, Lottie discerned the morning sounds of the neighbors which even Gus' meticulous trowel work could not deaden. In the yard below, Sabine was taking the clothes off the line, stacking Lottie's in one basket, and her own in another, as if the fine should not mingle with the coarse. This pleased Sabine, doing chores for her older sister.

In return, Lottie patiently listened to stories of home, delivered with little imagination, embellished with longing. She resented being pulled backwards into their joint past and strained towards a future of unshared space. What held Lottie here was the belief that her presence protected her sister from Gus, that martyr to civility. Sabine was afraid of him. Of what wasn't she afraid?

A house of their own was out of the question. All of Lottie's heroic efforts to support them at the camp were simply making do now, with no prospects, as far as she could see, for change. She no longer kept a ledger, that record an indictment of her meager progress. She would just have to think harder.

The Jevell driver was singing his way up the alley, calling out to the women to buy his detergent. The sisters often joked about the men in their lives. Louie, who brought the eggs and whose pockets always held a candy bar or two, would join them for a cup of coffee. From the peddler who came once a week with his sample case of lace undergarments--so adept at appealing to her as a woman of discerning taste--Lottie always bought more than she could afford.

"This week I'm going to stay in my room," she threatened.

"He'll get the wrong idea." Sabine didn't wish to offend anyone. The peddler reminded her of their mother's selling efforts, the walk each week to town and back, the wagon weighed down with fabric or goods. Lottie had given up on her own sewing, leaving Sabine to interpret matters of style for both of them.

The beer and soda man pulled up, the truck bumper grazing one of Gus' stone pillars. Sabine abandoned the wash to carry out the case of empty bottles. Lottie called down that she would help, welcoming the diversion.

Today, as he did every Wednesday, the scissor grinder opened up shop on the back of his truck. About four, the Italian greengrocer arrived with his horse and cart in time for them to haggle over the price of the vegetables for dinner. And then Gus, that specialist in the art of making plaster resemble stone, came home with his brushes in his satchel. Rudy sometimes late because he didn't have regular hours or work, which was fine because then he and Lottie had an excuse to eat alone. Afterwards, if it wasn't too dark, they would sit on the porch smoking and waiting, along with the children, for the arrival of Bungalow Pete, who dispensed his ice cream confections from a truck in the shape of a house.

9

The car paused as if hung up on something, then flipped over once, twice, before righting itself. It gave a shudder, and then was still.

So this was what it felt like. A falling and ascending at the same time, fear rising from the stomach to meet the pain in the chest. How he imagined the sensation if one day the straps broke. Rudy's first impulse was to tighten every muscle but willed his body to go limp; it was almost a relief to let himself be thrown, tumbled about.

Only the driver was involved in the mishap, but from the moment the vehicle left the road, Lottie was in the passenger seat beside him. Rudy knew she would be helpless before the sight of someone else's pain.

"She would never be able to stand this," he thought.

His arm had gotten twisted somehow; gingerly he tested its limits. Touch carefully. A little pain here, a lot of pain there. Definitely the ribs and who knew what else. Not the arm, thank goodness. A bad wrist sprain at worst. Lottie would have had other concerns. She wouldn't have held her tongue for long.

"You were always lucky, Rudy. Now do something about your face."

The shivering started almost immediately, the body's way to keep warm.

"Those blankets would come in handy about now. They must be strewn all over the road. Quality stuff, too. Last a lifetime. Fetch a good price in New York, bring in a little income."

Not that things went badly with them, what with Lottie's investments and Rudy working off the books.

"So much for this little venture. So much for an extra week in Europe. On me for a change. Wouldn't that have been something?"

He had tried the lawn business. Too seasonal. Besides, how could a man maintain a sense of dignity on his knees? All right, he had to admit, hanging from a building wasn't much better, a stick figure with one arm extended, straining against the belt with nothing but air under him.

"I suppose I could tell her I swerved to avoid hitting a jack rabbit. She might buy that, animal lover that she is. Or lay the blame on Willy. All his fault. Well, to be honest, Willy was about fifth down the line. Fish. Pierre. A toast to each of them. One led to another. To the Cook. And to his sweet wife. Quiet woman. Fortunate Cook. I bet she'd have plenty to say, though, if he cracked up her car. Sharpen those knives of hers. I should have stayed. She insisted. Should have been sensible. Listened and stayed. For another round, for another toast to the old days.

"Try lifting the legs. Got to get out of the car. But then what? Hitchhike. No one would stop for something looking like this. I should clean myself up. Wouldn't want to scare them. Did you ever notice how they never look you in the eyes, just speed up as they drive by? Must extricate myself. Drag my tail home. Only one thing to do and that's to put the best face possible on this little disaster."

Rudy grinned, tasted blood on his lips, rubbed his good arm across his forehead, checking out the source.

"One thing I know I mustn't do. And that's to tell Lottie the truth."

"You were drinking, admit it. No, I don't want to hear excuses."

She would spend a long time with that, hoping for a bit of satisfaction to chew on. Maybe long enough to divert her from other, less obvious issues.

"You're not going to like it. That's okay. We've moved past this point many times. But, just how much will you put up with? You always thought I was testing you. Probably not. At least I don't think so. You don't even come into it sometimes. Lots of times. Better not tell you that. I don't think about you all the time. You're not foremost on my mind. Ha! Here you are now, ready to contradict me."

He began to cry, not for his broken body but because her face was going to look that way again, as if he had struck her.

Lottie clutched the tile edge of the sink; for an instant she felt as if the linoleum under her feet had shifted. She had a premonition that Rudy was injured, or worse, dead; it took physical shape, a weakness in her legs. She was alone upstairs, a visitor in her sister's house. Sabine was in the basement making soap. Lottie had a strong impulse to call out, but didn't. Sabine would believe her. Sabine would share the worry, magnify it. Better to say nothing. Lottie sat down at the table. The coffee was still warm. She pushed her ring finger in and out of the handle of the glass cup and wondered why the hot liquid didn't crack it and why, at times like this, she was drawn to food. She took a bite of the doughnut, the powdered sugar catching in her throat; for an instant Lottie suspected she might be choking, the possibility almost making her happy.

She had wanted to go along, threatening not to give him any money for the trip, but Rudy was insistent. She might have been able to help. Or she might now be dead, herself. She could have been more definite that he not travel alone. It was her car, after all. Everytime he got behind the wheel she expected bad news. She would never know what really happened. Sabine would say that was a blessing.

"I'll write, that's what I'll do. That way it won't come as such a shock. Like a bolt out of the blue." Here Rudy imagined a blue flash coming down through the fireplace, which they never could use, striking Lottie in the apartment, surprising her where she thought she was safest.

"I'll tell her I was just driving along, thinking about getting home, and this bolt of lightning came down from the sky and slammed into the hood of the Studebaker. Better yet, the tire blew out and, before I knew it, I'd landed in this ravine. Well, hardly a ravine. A deep gully at best. Now, just pray it doesn't rain. Flash flood. This could get more serious. Hard to swim with a couple of broken ribs. Hard to breathe. Easy, breathe easy. Shallow breaths so it doesn't hurt so much.

"I think I'm going to put my head down on this wheel and take a little snooze. Just a little while. Relax. Get your voice out of my head."

"Tell me, Rudy, this is as bad as it's going to get. Don't tell me. Swear it. For once, just once, make me a promise. One you won't go back on. I've never asked the impossible, never begged you to stop drinking. Just don't let it get any worse.

I'm pretty confident I can take this, whatever 'this' turns out to be, but I'm not so sure if something worse comes along."

"There were other, minor accidents, my dear. Nothing worth mentioning. A little green paint on the rear fender where I'd nicked a parked car. A dog." That he would never tell her about. The animal had bluffed and lost, dashing across the road at the last minute.

"No, no promises. Don't insist or I'll be forced to lie. Hush, woman. I don't want to hear it. Not now. It takes two people to make an argument and one of us is going to sleep." He put his head on the wheel.

When Rudy woke in the hospital there were rough edges and the sheets hurt his ankles and wrist; when he tried to turn, the cloth wound around him until, no matter how hard he kicked, he couldn't work himself free. They had placed his arm in a casing impervious to all pressure; when he lay on his side, resting his entire weight on it, he felt nothing.

Even at those moments when his strength failed him, Rudy had it all straight in his head, just what he would say and how he would say it. But there was no one to practice on, no one to even pretend to believe him.

Lottie waited for Rudy to communicate with her; she had seldom waited for anything to happen to her in her life. Then, only this cryptic postcard: "Had an accident. Car totalled. Yours truly, almost." It was a relief. What she had so often imagined, finally happening. No more holding her breath. And he wasn't dead. But a postcard. Not even a phone call. At least he could have managed a few miserable pages.

She wished they'd been separated just shortly after they met. Those letters, full of longing, would have been worth saving. But never once had he written. If she had one now, she could read it and remember how it was between them. It would have been something to hang on to, something to keep against the bad days--and this surely qualified.

"Was there ever a time, Rudy," she thought, "when you weren't trouble?"

Lottie never forgave him for letting her know so late after the fact, when his face had already set, the scar like a thin crack in the smooth plaster of his forehead. He had shown up at the door to their apartment, blankets in his arms, offered up as some sort of reparation. What did he think she would do with them? Tie them together, lower them out the window and make her escape?

She was convinced he actually enjoyed her reaction, her breath catching at the first sight of him standing there. With no warning. A bolt out of the blue, her heart turning over and over like she was falling and nothing--no belt, or scaffold--to clutch at.

10

She had to lie to get the job. It was easier than she thought.

"Have you ever cooked for large groups of people?" the Captain of the Norwegian freighter inquired.

Surely a hundred conscientious objectors in a camp in Colorado, their appetites fueled by hard labor and the mountain air, would qualify. And the words, "auxiliary cook" had a nice, if sufficiently vague, sound to them; the Captain was impressed.

"We're not so many people," he said. "You'll find our tastes quite simple." Take a recipe for four, double it, add half again as much. How difficult could the job be?

As to the question of whether or not she became seasick, Lottie only shrugged her shoulders, her experiences off shore limited to fishing in shallow water. As she and her nieces ate candy bars, Gus slowly rowed, the lines becoming tangled. Thin grey specters flicked along the silty bottom, frying pan size.

"Just drop the sinker on their noggins," their father instructed his squeamish daughters, pushing sandworms onto the hooks. It was one of the few times Lottie found the man almost endearing.

Prepare fish: poached, boiled or baked. That she could do. Filet them first, not so deftly accomplished. But in time, with practice, that, too.

For Lottie's first meal the steward had set the table with a battery of cutlery and china as though it were a special occasion. There were the requisite fish knives with ivory handles. And butter knives. The spoons--dessert, coffee and soup-- were placed face down between the water and wine glasses. The table was littered with coasters and salt cellars. The ponderous china bore the ship's insignia; heavy to withstand the rough seas, she thought.

For the main course that evening she had chosen fish in a puddle of white sauce, a cream base, tasting better than it looked and, because of a miscalculation on her part, stretched with noodles. To a man, they had seconds.

The steward made a face as he set the plate down in front of her; the Captain had insisted Lottie take off her apron and join them.

"We're starved for female companionship," he said.

The steward wasn't a bad fellow, a boy really. He was just homesick. It was potato pancakes he missed, and when she made him a batch, he came around.

The Nescafé jar sat on a saucer in the middle of the table. When the Captain reached for the spoon, it was a signal that the meal was over; out came the cigarettes and scotch. After that evening, Lottie made a fresh pot of coffee with every meal, thick with egg shells to settle the grinds, filling a thermos for those still on duty. It was easy to spoil agreeable fellows who accepted whatever was placed before them without complaint. Lottie went out of her way to please them; it had been a long time since she made an effort to please anyone.

The boys were becoming fast friends, but once on land, they scattered and went their separate ways, some to buy uncut gemstones for their wives and sweethearts, others to forget them. But they always knew where to find her, in the markets, bartering, loading up on whatever produce was freshest, sampling that aspect of the local culture. When the ship laid over and took on cargo for more than one day, Lottie bought bowls, dishes and flowers in riotous colors to offset the somber white linens. It was as if, like a new bride, she was furnishing a household.

When she asked about the men's favorite foods, knowing the recipes would be almost impossible to duplicate, the Captain responded, "We can get those dishes at home. Fix us your specialty."

She inquired if his wife was a good cook. The captain said he kept a farm in the North above the Arctic Circle; one day he would return to Norway and live there with his mother. Lottie wondered about a man who had never married, now already in his forties.

The first few days out of port, they feasted. Several courses: soup, fresh greens and vegetables. Each day the remains went into one pot, the stew becoming richer and more potent as they got further away from land. Ingredients were contributed from the larder: some tinned fish, canned vegetables. The exotic flowers died and Lottie harvested the seeds for Sabine.

There was always dessert. Usually a sponge cake, the batter light and not so sweet, but filled with canned fruit after the fresh had spoiled because she always bought too much, the syrup boiled down and carmelized, whipped cream on the side for those who wished it. She dreamt of raspberries, strawberries, berries of every kind. Tarantulas curled about the bananas in the hold.

The Spark complained about his waistline. "We'll not all fit on the bridge." He was easily bored and often roamed from his post, seeking company in the galley.

"Like a bear after the honey," the Captain said, winking at Lottie. If he spoke sternly to the men, she never heard it.

The night was the best time, the evening chores behind her, the table set for the next day's breakfast. Lottie switched off the light; the cockroaches scuttled across the countertops. She took her coffee out on deck. Being on the ship was like inhabiting an illuminated house sited on dark ground; when you looked out you saw only what was reflected back from the light of the moon. There was no fixed reference point, although the Captain had introduced her to the coordinates and named the stars. The steadfast Captain, who kept his own counsel and course.

It was hard to imagine another world outside of this ongoing passage. Barely the sensation of movement, no sound but that of the engines; just the wake gave their forward motion away. She had difficulty at such times recalling Rudy's face as it used to be. Lottie tried not to think of the sorry state he would be in when she reached home, although he was always grateful to see she had returned as promised. He would be kind the first few days, on his best behavior. He would take her face in his hands; she could remember the hands. For a moment, the engines were hushed, idle before resetting themselves and pushing on; in that second, they were adrift, perhaps even floating backwards.

She lifted her arm from under the Captain's head. "Don't smoke in bed. Please," she said.

This concession he made to her, among others. He asked for little; it was easy for her to gratify his desires, as if taking into bed a friend in need of some elemental comfort. The sex was just one more gift offered, like the cakes or the cup of freshly-ground coffee. Lottie didn't fool herself; there had been other cooks. But there was delight in the unconditional acceptance of the gift, by inference, a nonjudgmental attitude about the way she conducted her life.

But, sometimes, in the cabin, she felt as if someone were holding a knifeblade against her breastbone and she couldn't breathe for fear of injuring herself. This happened if she dwelt too long on how far she had been carried towards a warmer climate. But then, she was quick to remember, one life was kept strictly apart from the other with little danger of overlap. Really, Lottie congratulated herself, she was a fortunate woman.

But when the ship docked, she was uneasy, examining herself in the glass. The voyage had marked her, although she appeared no heavier or thinner. On her face she thought she detected the look of a woman secure in the knowledge she'd been putting something over on someone else.

If her husband noticed, he didn't let on. He was sober. He was glad to have his wife home. Glad for the presents. From the bag containing the cigarettes, those smuggled past the customs agent, the cockroach emerged, making straight for the cabinet under the sink, seeking a land base, merging the two parts of her life she had meant to keep separate.

11

For Gus, the women were solace; they made everything bearable. There seemed to be no end to them. They were the sort who openly appreciated the meticulous care he took in his appearance, who knew where the fun was, but had the good sense never to ask him to dance. Women who had learned not to expect too much from life, self taught in the art of concealing disappointment.

Once Gus thought he had been in love. Her name was Nora. The two had kept company for several months. Almost everything she did was calculated to aggravate or tease; Nora seemed to take pleasure in his discomfort. She was good at games and ran Gus all over the tennis court. On the rides at Coney Island, he had no choice but to accept her challenge after she leapt first from the parachute jump. She enjoyed dancing in crowded places, but Gus didn't like the way she swung away from him on the floor, for one suspenseful moment letting go of his hand, until he yanked her back in close. He preferred dark movie theatres where she couldn't so openly invite admiration.

After a day spent together, Gus was happy to say his farewells, relieved of the effort to stay one step ahead of his companion. Within the week, he had called again. Nora would feign indifference; she had a rehearsal, or was going to meet friends. When she sensed he had suffered enough, she invited him to her apartment and cooked a meal his sisters would never have attempted, the entrée spice laden, the dessert something set aflame.

The sisters didn't care for Nora. She was untidy in her person, incorporating bits of her onstage costume into her everyday apparel. They were waiting for someone to take over the care of their brother's laundry, the two changes of underwear and fresh shirts he required each day.

Sabine was invited out to Queens, ostensibly to visit with Gus' mother, whom she had met aboard ship. Imperious, hawklike, and astute, the old woman had swooped down on the unsure girl as a likely prospect for her son.

At lunch, Sabine was seated across from Gus. He admired the way she ate, dabbing at the corners of her mouth with the napkin. Afterwards, she helped clear the plates. They played badminton, Gus appraising his partner over the net. She wasn't a natural athlete, but threw herself into the game and was graciously accepting of her losses. She remarked on his skill. Gus trounced his guest easily and mercilessly.

"Enough," he said. Sabine put down her racquet. It was clear she would defer to him on more important decisions. It wasn't clear whether she would see him again; she thought him a bit of a show off.

Gus approached Nora with a box in his breast pocket and an ultimatum. While he was not yet ready to commit to settling down, he definitely wanted to constrict her activities. If he had any real understanding of the obstinate nature of the woman he loved, he might not have miscalculated so badly. Nora's response was to take off with the troupe when they went on the road. Gus' sister, Hedwig, persuaded him not to return the ring.

"You never know," she said, teasing, "when such a thing might come in handy."

Gus and Sabine were married and moved to Queens, a short block from the sisters who could better supervise their brother's care. The couple did not have a honeymoon; Sabine never made it to Niagara Falls. Gus did carry his bride over the threshold of their new house, and they spent a weekend moving in Sabine's belongings. They ate out once and went to a movie.

The borough of Queens was as far out in the country as Gus dared venture from his job. Sabine, in later years, when she still had Hans and Lottie to back her up, would remind her husband that he was a farm boy; her family had been city people and, presumably, closer to the seat of culture.

Sometimes a wife of one of his employers, who remained in her Manhattan apartment during the day to keep the workmen honest, would offer Gus a beverage to go along with the sandwiches he carried in his leather satchel, inviting him into the kitchen and making the coffee herself after dismissing the maid. Gus was always careful to make his excuses after the half-hour break was up, often interrupting a torrent of complaint about an absent husband. Secretly, he didn't have much respect for these men who, in spite of their schooling, could do nothing practical with their hands.

Later, after his surgery, when the young girls no longer brushed up against him on the subway, Gus met women in bars. Unkempt women, who issued their challenges, after pulling the stool closer, in hushed tones. He never sought them out and was careful not to ask personal questions. He always felt he didn't misrepresent his intentions, that he didn't hold out any false promises. Somehow these edgy encounters made it easier to haul the satchel home, up the street with its dark canopy of leaves. His children would be playing under the street lamps, having already eaten dinner. If their father's appearance happened to coincide with the arrival of the ice cream truck, they would tap him for a couple of dimes. Otherwise, after a casual salute, they skated off with their friends, whose own fathers were fed and watching t.v. safely inside. It was easy to get cynical, Gus thought sadly, about one's own children.

They were too passionate in their play; Sabine, Tessa and Charlotte always seemed to be celebrating some occasion from which he was excluded. The front door heralded the approach of another holiday; shamrocks were pasted to the small square of stained glass. Sometimes it was rabbits, or hearts. At Christmas, a handmade wreath. One Halloween Sabine had hung a jack-o-lantern made of cardboard. It swung back and forth each time the door was opened or closed; the electric bulb glowed through the paper sides and Gus complained he was going to trip on the wire.

"I suppose," Sabine said, "it would kill you to say something nice."

By the time he showered, changed, creamed his hands, and played with the parakeet, the dinner had been warmed over so many times his wife had to keep adding water to the pot. She set the plate of misshapen food in front of him and then disappeared, leaving Gus to eat alone. When she began to be afraid of the tight knot forming in her chest where her heart used to be, and wanting to soften her feelings towards him, Sabine sat down to commiserate.

"Saying goodbye to your parents for the last time must have been difficult."

At such times Gus would look at his wife as if he hadn't a clue as to what she was talking about.

"Where did that come from?" he asked.

He never spoke about work anymore because something about the women might slip out, although he hinted broadly enough. When he intimated as much in front of the children, Sabine said, "Pop likes to blow his own horn." How many small victories had he managed without her encouragement?

She never could see what he envisioned for this place. Look what he'd had to start with. Nothing but rocks. Patiently, he raked and pried them out. He built up the soil, adding sawdust, peatmoss and sand to the loam he carried back from the woods in the wheelbarrow. He had built the fish pond and edged everything neatly with a wall made from those same boulders. The small victory garden the city had allowed him was fenced in to keep out rabbits and the neighbor's goat. Gus built a shed to house his gardening tools, nailed up a lattice trellis and laid down gravel paths. It was a painful surprise when the city sold the property; he had improved the land and came to regard it as his own. Too early, long before his retirement, after he had covered every inch of soil in the garden with bulbs, trees and bushes and painted all the surfaces of the house in imitation of more costly materials, Gus ran out of space, his ambition outgrowing the square footage allotted it.

His youngest daughter stood in front of him clutching a cardboard box with a ragged hole cut into the front panel: a puppet theatre, part of her class project to depict Washington crossing the Delaware. Tessa reminded her father, again, that he had promised to help with the painting. She had done as much as she could on her own, cutting out and dressing the cardboard figures, fashioning a crude boat. She knew enough not to mess with Gus' tools. It was late, past her bedtime, but she had waited up for him. Tessa's voice took on a panicked, insistent tone. She sat on the workbench impatiently opening and closing the vise, while her father stirred the color, a salmon pink, left over from an apartment on the upper East Side. He methodically instructed her in the correct way to apply the brush strokes. The cardboard soaked up the paint so that it wasn't dry by the time she did the lettering. It wasn't dry when she carried the box to school the next morning, holding it unsuccessfully away from her clothing, smearing the words into illegibility. The teacher gave her a high mark; it was clear this student had attempted something a bit more ambitious than the other children's two-dimensional efforts, without, obviously, any parental assistance.

The family learned to function around Gus' absences with mixed success. Sabine pushed Edward on the swing at the park and spoke to the other mothers in the voice of a single parent. But she wouldn't join in the general lament about the lock on the front door that went unrepaired, or the leak under the sink.

She said, brightly, thinking of the roster of brothers-in-law and trades at her disposal, "Do what I do, call someone."

But, impatient, Sabine had painted the trellis herself.

"You almost killed the roses." Gus had the last word on his wife's handiwork. Obviously, his family didn't have the same commitment to perfection. By now their Christmas traditions had come to include Gus dragging home a tree he had bought at the last moment, a spindly reject. From the basement he fetched his tools, the saw and drill, and proceeded to rearrange the branches, lopping off one and moving it higher or lower, then another, until the entire tree was remade to his satisfaction. He stood aside in triumph, oblivious to the maimed bark and fallen needles.

"It won't look so bad," Sabine said, "after the tinsel goes on."

Nothing Gus could do would make his wife or daughters respect or love him enough, not even later when he designed and built his own house, teaching himself, from books, how to do the plumbing and wiring. A man who would tackle such an undertaking! And with such looks! Somehow the accolades never came. Well, if they couldn't see it, he knew of other, more appreciative women, whose words of praise didn't stick in their throats, but sprang, parrotlike and unbidden, from their full, red lips.

12

This feeling took some getting used to. Not that there weren't moments, here and there. On summer days, Sabine flung the hose over the trellis out back and she and the girls ran through the icy spray, squealing. Delicious, first the chill, then stepping out into the warming sun, followed by reimmersion into the shock of the cold. To replicate it, she had only to turn on the water.

This was different, a largesse that embraced not only the members of her family, but complete strangers as well. She was its center, its source. Sabine, who hated to get out of bed in the mornings, now seemed to require less sleep. After standing on her feet at work, she returned home, her step buoyant. She no longer flinched whenever her husband entered the room, no longer backed down from an argument. Nor would she provoke one. If Gus was late yet again for supper, she made no complaint, not even to her sister.

"What's up?" Lottie asked, suspicious.

When pressed, Sabine refused to find fault with her new job, in spite of the hours, which were expanding to take up most Saturdays. In the bakery she moved with ease between kitchen and counter; she was good at the till and enjoyed gossiping with the regular customers. Of her employer, Mr. Shea, a portly man with prematurely white hair, Sabine would only remark, "Kurt and I are sympathetic to one another," even after she had begun to find him attractive. She did not go on about his many kindnesses.

Lottie was sure to tease, "You'd run off with the first salesman who came to the door if he spoke a sweet word to you."

It was never a question of running off. Never that.

Sabine hurried to work without eating breakfast, wanting
to see Kurt before he retired to the small room at the head of
the stairs. She had never seen the inside, the cot where he slept,
did not allow herself to picture it. The smell of coffee greeted
her. Kurt filled the cup brimming with milk the way she liked
it. Sabine buttered two rolls. She talked about the time Hans,
her brother, had been a baker, as if that were reason enough
for their friendship. She told Kurt about her life in Germany,
her guilt at having left her father, a widower, for the second
time. He saw how easily others had manipulated that soft
heart, would have been surprised to be accused of doing the
same. He was attentive, alert for a sign that Sabine understood
they weren't merely passing the time before the first customers
came through the door, but sharing an intimate breakfast like
some married couple.

She liked the way he listened, searching her face, as if he
looked deep inside and approved of what he saw there, no
matter that her hair, so carefully wound up in pins the night
before, had straightened to her shoulders, or that the dress was
the same she had worn the previous day. Most of all she liked
knowing he was upstairs while she worked, that, even asleep,
he watched over her.

Sabine worked Tuesdays now, half a day. The second
Tuesday of each month, the health inspector showed up with
his hand out for the bag of danish, for the envelope.

"Otherwise," Kurt said, "he might conveniently find rats
in the basement."

This angered Sabine in a way she had never been angry for

herself. Kurt was weak for giving in; that's what Gus would say. But he would have paid, too, only making sure no one, least of all his wife, ever witnessed the transaction.

The week stretched out long between Tuesday and Saturday. Sabine didn't like to think of Kurt working the evening shift alone. At five o'clock, he came downstairs to lock up before he started the baking. At those moments, when he rested his hand on Sabine's shoulder before bidding her good night, she forgot about the two girls waiting eagerly at home for yesterday's black forest cake, the cream gone a little off. Once the plain, compact center of those ingenuous lives, she didn't care to know of Charlotte's narrow escape after her best friend had maliciously emptied bees into their milkbox. Or that her youngest, Tessa, huddled behind the billboard on the highway with a cache of stolen cigarettes, attempted to blow the perfect smoke ring.

Summer weekends Gus went alone to the vacation house he was building; he couldn't understand how his children preferred running under the garden hose to swimming in salt water. At the bakery, Sabine gave the girls the task of cleaning the glass on the display cases; as a reward, they were allowed to fill the donuts. Tessa pierced the centers of each ball of dough on the cross bars of the pump and pushed down, once, twice, until the jelly oozed out. These she claimed as her own.

Mr. Shea protested, "You'll bankrupt me," but smiled.

As long as nothing was acknowledged, as long as he and Sabine pretended to be what they no longer were, employer and employee, it was safe to be in the presence of the children. At five o'clock, because the relief baker came in the early hours of Sunday, Kurt's day off, he drove them home, but never went inside, even in Gus' absence, abiding by rules Sabine was making up as she went along.

Free of husband and the conflicting emotions at work, she packed a picnic for their Sunday dinner and took the girls to the woods, the last remaining stand of trees in the neighborhood. She shared the lemonade with Mr. John, the old man who had once lived on the farm there; he sat on an overturned kerosene can while, over their heads, Tessa and Charlotte straddled the limbs of a choke cherry tree. He, too, liked to talk about how much better things used to be. For once, Sabine disagreed.

Mr. Shea invited her to his summer place, "That means your husband and children as well."

Gus went unwillingly, but became more enthusiastic when he saw that the house sat on a canal and he could do some fishing. To Sabine, the building appeared like a ship moored at its berth, the white superstructure heavy with balconies. Husband and wife slept on the top floor in a bedroom with high ceilings, the sheer curtains blowing at the windows, which were kept open at night. The children delighted in climbing into the dumb waiter which connected their room to the pantry. Sabine pretended they were in an elegant hotel where she knew the proprietor personally, although she was startled to see a picture of a man confidently astride a horse, obviously a younger, slimmer Mr. Shea, and wondered what else she did not know about him. Gus, too, succumbed to the holiday mood and became amorous; under the circumstances, Sabine thought she couldn't refuse him. But when she admired the marble tiles on the bathroom floor--the black squares spelling out the word, BAIN, set into the shape of a mat before the tub, each of whose claw feet gripped a green marble--Gus said it was just an old place poorly wired and with outdated plumbing. The pipes bellowed when they turned on the hot water tap; the lights flickered over the table as they played cards in the evening.

"Spooks," Charlotte said.

Kurt showed the girls how to wrap the heads of roosters in old nylon stockings--their mother wondered on whose legs they had been worn--and swing the bait over the edge of the dock. He scooped up the crabs in a net and boiled them on the big gas stove in the kitchen. He showed Charlotte where to grab them so they wouldn't pinch with their claws, but Tessa refused to watch as they were thrown into the huge enamel pot. On the cavernous porch, under Kurt's tutelage, Sabine shelled the crabs for salad. It seemed natural that he helped with the dinner preparations; after all, Gus had often said that the best chefs in the world were men.

Kurt took the girls out in his small sailboat; Sabine sensed he was careful they were never alone together.

"You know how to do this, right?" he asked Gus, when it was his turn. "Just stay in the bay," he cautioned, "and you two will be fine."

Sabine assumed from the manner in which her husband fiddled with the ropes on the dock that he was an experienced sailor. She was nervous that the water came almost to the rails as they stepped aboard the shallow craft, but then, their guardian hovered nearby. Gus assumed his wife would be as much a helpmate at sea as she was on land.

At first all went reasonably well; Sabine confined herself to staying out of the range of the boom, whose sail chattered overhead. When they had difficulty tacking, she held her tongue. The wind teased at the sails and Gus let out the sheet, planting his feet more firmly. Soon they were heading out to open water, passing beyond the protection of the spit of land on which the house sat, beyond all reach of Kurt to save them. The water slapped against and over the sides. Her hair and face wet, Sabine insisted they turn around. "Now!" Her voice became shrill. Gus ignored his wife as the boat fought his efforts to come about. Sabine clutched the picnic hamper to her chest and screamed. It startled them both. Throwing up his hands in disgust, Gus let go of the lines; they were no longer going anywhere. He sat down in a puddle on the floor of the boat, and crossed his arms. It was the first time, ever, that he felt clumsy around the water. Sabine began to unload the hamper, thinking to appease her husband with a crab sandwich or a donut.

An Indian, whose people had once owned the land under Mr. Shea's house, had been observing the sailboat's uneven progress through a pair of binoculars; he came towards them now in a skiff powered by an outboard motor. In his efforts to secure a line to their bow, his boat glided out from under him until the man's body was stretched across the open water between the two vessels. His pants, which had been fastened casually with a rope, fell down. Little creatures were imprinted on his shorts: running deer. Even this burlesque couldn't distract Gus, so obsessed was he with his own humiliation.

On land, Kurt observed that his guests were in no real danger, but then Gus looked like the sort of man who would take out his misery on his wife. At least Gus waited until they all got into the car, but not quite out of the driveway, which went on for an impressive stretch before it intersected the road.

· · ·

Perhaps, flying over, the flock of wild swans had been lured into believing that the temporary puddles in the field were a wild marsh; the trumpeters' necks rose between the play equipment while, nearby, traffic rushed towards the beaches. For some reason, this sight struck Sabine as unbearably sad.

The lake was shunned by the swans; they weren't taken in by its luminous face. Up close, it was muddy and shallow, choked with algae and water lilies that never bloomed. A steep hill rose from its center. Humans reclined in the shallow pockets of stunted grass. Beer bottles floated on the water's surface. Kurt apologized. He said he hadn't been to this park in years. He thought the girls would enjoy it, enjoy spending Sunday together. Sabine knew this was risky. Her well being now required Kurt's constant presence.

They were wedged together in the small boat, eating their sandwiches, tipping over the thermos of lemonade, tangling fishing lines in the oars. They pulled in a couple of perch and threw them back again. The girls wanted to explore the island.

"Maybe there are snakes," Charlotte said.

Kurt seemed to welcome the opportunity to stretch his legs, but as soon as the girls scampered up the side, he got back into the boat, and shoved off.

"You row," he ordered Sabine. "Please," he added.

The gnats drove them away from the shore. Once in awhile Sabine pulled on the oars and they gained a few yards, but then drifted again, at the mercy of the wake of the motorboats.

"We've got too much weight in here," Kurt said. She

started to protest, but he waved his hand. "Well, what can you expect from a man in my business?" he laughed.

Kurt joined her on the thwart, and after a time, their rowing motions became less erratic, taking on a rhythm of their own, although he had to stop once in awhile to compensate for being the stronger. He put one hand on Sabine's knee and pulled the oar with the other. She put her hand over his. For awhile, the boat bumped against the island.

Sabine knew this contentment, coupled with a slight tension, couldn't last; her desires alone weren't sufficient to sustain it. Her new-found sense of independence, that she no longer felt indebted to her husband, was inextricably tied to her job. And now here was Mr. Shea confirming her worst fears by announcing his early retirement. In his businesslike voice, or so it seemed to her, he told Sabine he was going to sell the bakery.

For "health reasons," for "other reasons." The pressure of his hand increased.

She wouldn't allow him to continue to speak. She began calling for the girls, shouting their names; suddenly, she had a great need to see them. Sabine felt this must be accomplished before she would allow herself to think of anything else. Circling the island, they came upon a man sitting cross-legged under a tree, listening to an opera broadcast. He shook his head; he had seen no children.

Sabine thought her family needed these separations once in awhile. At least that's what she had been telling herself lately. After several minutes time, however, she thought the girls were gone for good, that somehow they had gotten off the island unseen and had chosen to live without her. What she had often imagined and secretly desired had now happened, but she felt no sense of freedom, merely panic.

The reality was Tessa and Charlotte, incredibly small, waving their arms from the top of the island, not in greeting, but urgently as if they needed their mother to come to their rescue. Impatient, they started their treacherous descent without her; all she could do was to worry them down the slope.

Crowded together again in the boat, the girls were arguing over whose turn it was to row. Gus, Sabine realized, would have become agitated and bullied them into silence. Charlotte took over first, then Tessa was rowing, bringing them in. Kurt told her when to raise the oars, "Now!" and they glided over the sand and got stuck, a bit short of the mark.

"Perfect," he said. "Our feet won't even get wet."

No barking of orders, no heroic actions, or bodies flinging themselves about; the sense of loss was overwhelming. Sabine looked out at the lake wishing to have her wretchedness confirmed in its polluted waters. All across the surface the late afternoon sun had been caught and fractured into a glitter of disks so brilliant she had to shield her eyes. In recollection, it would always be like this, a false beauty.

Unloading the boat, carrying the cushions and life jackets, they passed an old Chevrolet, its doors and trunk open as if the car was airing itself. A radio competed with the strains of "Die Meistersinger" coming from the island. On the hood, two teenagers entwined in a snarl of slender arms and pale legs were oblivious to their passage, the clumsy maneuvering of the boat on its trailer, the jabbering voices of the girls. Sabine imagined the metal must be hot.

She felt sorry for herself. Sorry for her children. This day would become a fragmented memory. Mr. Shea would merely be a name to them, someone who passed briefly through their lives. No more than Mr. John, unless she told them the old man was dying of cancer; only then would they become enamoured of the tragic details of his life.

At this moment, she mustn't give herself away, hint at any disappointment, another one of her rules, because the girls might sometime, in innocence, seemingly when all danger was past, bring up Kurt's name, even tease her about him a little. Sabine didn't think she could bear to recreate her present pain or be reminded of its source, the result of misplaced, foolish trust, a momentary lapse into the delusion that here was happiness.

13

A rigid grid, defined by adult prejudice, was superimposed on the civic pattern of avenues and streets of the old neighborhood. Blacks were exiled in two asbestos-shingled multi-family houses where 50th Avenue swerved to sever 61st Street. The attached brick homes of Czechs, Germans, Italians and other Middle Europeans jostled each other with grudging familiarity on the street's upper end. Jews, of whatever nationality, inhabited the lower. Despite parental warnings, the children, on their skates, ranged defiantly over the lines.

Tessa still bore an indentation at her temple; the boy had lobbed the rock from the recesses of the apartment yard. Sabine complained, and all parties were brought face to face in the principal's office. Even the rhyme about the pimple in Mrs. Kelly's belly, repeated over and over in Tessa's head, did nothing to diminish the woman's authority. Or her own guilt at having muttered the obscenity, which instigated the attack. In the end, it came down to Tessa's word against the boy's. When each child was reprimanded in turn, Gus was indignant; there must have been provocation. It was inconceivable that both versions of the truth be given equal weight.

Tessa was less brave when running past the last of the houses on 61st Street to get to the candy store on the corner, afraid of catching something, afraid of being caught. This was where Pearl Mother lived. On a block peopled with exotic faces, hers startled, dark hair pulled back fiercely to reveal ears like tiny shells.

The widow, Mrs. Perlmutter, craved anonymity. Her house was overgrown with vegetation. Vines encircled the windows, the front door barricaded behind two dense yew bushes. The cracks in the sidewalk out front sprouted weeds. Cats preened themselves on the stoop, but Pearl Mother was never seen tending to them or watering the plants which thrived in the heat of summer. Even in winter, heat seemed to come from that house.

On the north side, the bricks were crumbling under the work of the ivy. A narrow alley ran along the side and back of the row of houses, defined by a steep wall: the children's escape route. From two small windows on this exposed side, Tessa imagined Pearl Mother observed them at their play in the empty lot, which was a dumping ground and a good place to explore, all the more inviting by its proximity to danger.

The vacant lot was full of cats, noisy and complaining. No one ever petted them and they got booted if they came too close. Wolfie tied the feet of one loosely to the end of a tree branch, then bent the limb and let it go like a catapult, sending the creature flying; he wanted to see if it would land on its feet. Tessa watched her cousin intently after that; she believed you were always punished for an unkind act. For disobedience. Her mother had warned her about sneaking to the candy store before dinner.

"If you do," she predicted, "you'll get sick."

Tessa threw up the ice cream on the way home, the mess lost in the debris of Good Humor sticks and gum wrappers in the curb fronting Pearl Mother's house. Dogs loved to hang around there, nosing after the cats.

Once, the older boys, like a bunch of thieving jays, roosted in Pearl Mother's cherry tree, gorging themselves.

"You damn kids," she hissed, "get out of that fucking tree."

None of their parents swore, at least in English; the tone of voice, more alarming than the invective, sent them scurrying for home.

Not far from Tessa's house, 61st Street ran up against Zion cemetery and became a dead end. The rows of headstones were jammed together like ill-fitting, black teeth. On Saturdays, the gates opened to let in lines of cars. The children never went in; something bad happened to nonbelievers who gained entry. If Pearl Mother had relatives there, they never saw her add to the piles of stones which grew higher on the more faithfully attended graves. On Sundays, toes anchored in the chain link fence, they reached over the top and knocked the stones off with their sling shots.

The twin smoke stacks of the incineration plant looked down on the oldest part of the cemetery, the garbage finding its way into the surrounding fields. Sitting in the weeds among the piles of tossed wallpapers, the children sifted through the fuzzy flockings, the shine of mylars. The keening rose like a chorus to accompany their play. It was louder than Charlotte's howls when she knelt on a broken beer bottle in the grass. The wailing continued over the leveling of the hill, the construction of a milk-processing plant, the unpopulated street along the cemetery now an avenue for the trucks that rumbled through day and night. The farmhouse was sacrificed, the choke cherry trees, all the cover, sending the tramps who sought shelter there to seek another hiding place. The collied monuments were the only permanence in the neighborhood; no one dared move the dead.

There was a funereal silence around Pearl Mother's house; no musical sounds other than the mewling of the cats in spite of the rumor that she gave piano lessons. The children of the neighborhood were all disciples of Miss Tuchman, who lived across the Boulevard. On Saturday mornings Tessa endeavored to coax her teacher's canary to sing. The pieces Miss Tuchman assigned were obscure classics, exercises in tortured fingering which her pupil couldn't master. Exasperated, she would wave the child off the bench, take charge of the instrument, and play the music with a heavy foot on the pedal, which Tessa was forbidden to use. Elsewhere in the house, Miss Tuchman's mother, the critic, also listened, the slamming of a kitchen drawer, or the scraping of a chair more eloquently damning than any bird's silence.

Cruel April came, time for the annual recital; Tessa's excuses about family commitments--weddings, trips to visit ailing relatives--fell on deaf ears. Miss Tuchman placed a call to Sabine, who cleared up any lingering doubts about the availability on that date. The invitations were sent out, the programs printed. The competitive tick of the metronome could be heard through the screen door of the house across the street where Tessa's friend, Martha, was being coached by her father. The theatre impresario had the foresight to change his daughter's last name to something less difficult to pronounce in anticipation of a career in show business.

He did not like Martha to play in the lots with the other children, putting her hands at risk. While away from the piano bench, the girls were witnesses to a man exposing himself on 63rd Street; Martha's mother called the police first and Martha got to tell them all about it. Tessa stood on the porch and looked dumbly at the police car parked importantly out in front of her friend's house. She didn't tell anyone about the man who rolled down the window of his car and said something about "directions." When that failed to draw her near, he had mouthed the word, "candy;" so this was what her mother had been going on so much about. Mesmerized, Tessa hung onto a tree to keep herself from giving in to a natural desire to see what was going to happen next. She never found out; a neighbor coming from the IGA grabbed her fiercely by the arm and pushed her towards home, repeating the license plate numbers over and over like a chant.

The parents didn't understand their children's fascination with the incineration plant, the cemetery, or 63rd Street, although they had seen stranger things. Once, a woman was found dead in front of the cemetery gates, deposited there with no clothes on. A man was thrown from a moving car, along with a pile of phonograph records and shoes, only the left ones. A week later, the right shoes appeared. Things like that happened mostly at night.

The photo on the front page of the newspaper showed five coffins, one large and four smaller, being carried down the steps of a church. A man across Laurel Hill Boulevard had locked himself up with his four children after his wife died. He wouldn't go on living without her and didn't want his children to be left without a mother or father. Tessa went into mourning and refused to come out and play. She wondered at the calmness with which the man had conceived and carried out his plan on the unsuspecting children whose names she noted and repeated in her prayers. She furnished the room where they all died; it was devoid of all decoration, even wallpaper, the furniture wooden and hard, to match the father's resolve. No grand piano stood in the corner covered by a fringed shawl--Tessa's idea of Pearl Mother's parlor, a more overwrought version of Miss Tuchman's, without the bird cage. Powerless to see into those two disparate interiors, Tessa invented spaces she could understand; these images fastened themselves to her dreams. She wondered what it would feel like to be orphaned, to be without this mother and father who failed to save her from recitals and encounters with the principal, who told her things she was beginning to suspect were not in her own best interest to believe.

On a day when she should have been practicing, Tessa and her friends were in the vacant lot next to Pearl Mother's house, pulling the stuffing out of an abandoned chair. Intent on their task, the children almost missed the black car back soundlessly out of the garage. The vehicle tried several times to negotiate the corner before it turned and headed up the side alley, stopping abruptly before it reached the street. The driver got out. Tessa could see the stockings and high-heeled shoes under the car on the other side, surprised they were not unlike those her mother wore. The woman knelt down beside the back tire and near-sightedly peered at the cat. She scooped up the animal, hugged it to her chest and let out a sound like a primitive echo of those cries they heard on Saturdays. Afraid to move, rooted to the spot, they were unwilling witnesses to such a naked display of grief. After what seemed like a very long time, Wolfie poked Tessa, "Let's get out of here."

"What are you kids doing? What are you looking at?"

Tessa saw the cat's limp head dangling from under Pearl Mother's arm, saw the look of hatred directed so openly at her; too late, she was cursed. Tessa took off at Wolfie's heels, felt her bare legs scratched by something.

She walked slowly past Pearl Mother's silent house after that, watching for the movement of curtains at the front windows. If the rituals were observed, you might avoid retribution; she placed a small stone on the wall in the alley.

The recital was held in Carnegie Hall, not the main stage, but imposing nevertheless. Sabine's present of lace handkerchiefs were a bribe to make up, in some way that they never could, for the wrenching ordeal ahead.

Harold Bronfman, a neighbor, drove them. Gus managed a well-practiced excuse, anticipating failure. When Miss Tuchman announced Tessa's name and selection, following Martha's flawless performance, Harold clapped vigorously.

Tessa sat down at the Steinway. The shaking began almost immediately in her knees and traveled upwards, settling into her hands, becoming not only visible but audible; the waltz opened with a curious staccato. She stared at the place where the sheet music should have been, and knew rote memory would never see her through. When the notes flew out of her head like a flock of routed birds, Tessa backtracked in an effort to retrieve them, playing over and over those she did remember, gathering momentum to make the leap across the gap in memory, instead of going on the way Miss Tuchman had advised. These bars of lapsed recollection appeared as walls against which she flung her fingers and then halted, starting over in yet another onslaught. It was like listening to someone learning to shift gears on a car.

At the end of the piece, more a faint drifting away of sound than a definite conclusion, Tessa's impulse was to flee, but she had to wait for the boy in his cap and uniform to bring her flowers down that endless aisle, tiger lilies cut from her father's garden. She stood there on stage, exhausted, with the pollen dusting the front of her new dress, exposed to the audience's polite and embarrassed applause, a prejudicial verdict about the finite possibilities of her life, the lines she might never successfully cross.

14

"Take 'em or leave 'em." The man at the tackle store refused to quibble about price.

The killies looked to Tessa as if they didn't have much life left in them. Her father paid without an argument. If she said anything, Gus would only remind her that when the bait was fresh, earlier in the day, she had been sound asleep. Charlotte emptied the machine of sodas and put them in a bucket of water; it was a hot day and all the ice had been sold. The only time they drank soda was when they fished. Even Gus drank it instead of his usual beer. Tessa bought three candy bars, but ate hers before it melted.

On the dock, a skate lay in their path. Charlotte prodded it with her foot. A ripple went through the creature, Tessa thought like a sigh; one fin moved, barely perceptible.

"It's alive," Charlotte said.

Gus placed his lit cigar in the fish's mouth; with each gasp of breath, it emitted a perfect circle of smoke. "How do you like that?" he said.

His daughters had seen the bellies of blow fish puff up under their father's insistent scratching.

Gus was comfortable on the water. His strong, shirtless back was hunched over the oars; he pulled them taut to his chest and the boat leapt forward. The wind blew them into a shallow grassy area and he set the motor, headed for the main channel, then cut the engine; they drifted back to where they started. He told the girls to put the lines over the sides.

They got no nibbles; the fluke and flounder seemed to prefer sandier bottom. Even with the motor going, Gus had to row to keep them from being blown further into shore. The rented boat needed caulking and they sat with their feet in water. Charlotte had hoarded her candy bar and began to eat it slowly in front of her sister. Tessa took a sandwich from the brown bag and offered her father the one with baloney, thick slabs of it, smothered in mustard. Charlotte and Tessa ate tea wurst, which was a paste that tasted nothing like its name, smeared on bread and washed down with the warm soda.

"Eating outside always makes you hungry," their father said, happily.

Between rowing and eating, they weren't getting much fishing done. Gus suggested they go to the ocean side for a swim.

They drove as tourists, craning their necks to see into the homes of the wealthy hidden behind sculpted hedges, wrought-iron gates and No Trespassing signs. A Spanish mansion, a Tudor pile, and the replica of a castle in Old Heidelberg sat exposed to the ocean, their dune covers eroded by the most recent hurricane. Further along the spit where the lawns blended into sea roses and wild grasses, the houses took on spare, geometric shapes and the potholes in the road became more serious. When the asphalt gave way to sand, they got out of the car.

Tessa wanted to stay on the inlet side, where the water was calmer. The jetty's arm sheltered a small warm pool and it was here she preferred to swim. There was always something to discover in the tidepools: barnacles, starfish, the shells of horseshoe crabs. Her father wanted to swim in the surf.

They headed across the dunes, single file, sending up clouds of angry birds; they rose up off their nests and flew out towards the water, regrouped, then returned, menacingly lower. Gus marched resolutely on, putting distance between himself and his children, while Charlotte and Tessa frantically waved their towels over their heads. Tessa was pleading, stumbling with eyes squeezed shut, her feet cut by broken shells.

"Shut up," Charlotte said, embarrassed.

They weren't alone. A camper was parked in the sand, the tarps on either end flapping in the wind. A tandem bicycle leaned against one of the tent poles. A dog, a golden retriever, was tied to another, straining at his leash. There was a swimmer in the water; once in awhile, an arm shot up out of the waves.

Gus pulled off his trousers, revealing his trunks. Tessa and Charlotte wrapped their towels around themselves and wiggled into their suits.

"Come on," their father coaxed.

Tessa had difficulty standing her ground as the retreating water sucked the sand from beneath her heels. Her legs felt like sticks, so much flotsam to be easily carried off. Gauging the next big wave, watching Charlotte pause, dive and head out with a strong breaststroke to meet the next one, Tessa made a half-hearted attempt at imitation. The sky, suddenly overcast, robbed her of courage. Plunging in, the shock of cold water was disorienting and she faltered, miscalculated and struck out for the beach. A wave broke over her head, sending her under and before she could struggle to her feet, another followed. Shaken, she limped to the blanket, hugging herself for warmth. She looked back, keeping Charlotte's pink cap, bobbing up and down on the swell, in her sight. In a panic, Tessa couldn't make out her father. Yes, there he was, treading water, calling out something to someone, her sister, or the other swimmer, she couldn't be sure.

The tide was coming in fast, nudging her back towards the dunes. She gathered up their belongings and shook out the blanket. A tern, flopping along the brown foam, made its way towards her, dragging a broken wing. The bird made frantic, pathetic sounds, "kee-aar, kee-aar." Tessa stood over it, kept her distance from the pointy black-tipped bill. She dropped the remains of a sandwich in its path but they were soon washed away. In the bird's eyes she read panic, its little heart, she imagined, beating faster and faster in fright.

She bent closer. "I wish I could help you, but I don't know what to do," she whispered.

Nothing to do but retract her looming presence, and leave the bird to continue its sad journey.

It didn't get far. The swimmer, a girl not much older than her sister, strode out of the water and stood with hands on her hips, blocking the tern's progress. She attempted to pick it up. It made a pass with its beak.

"Damn."

She lunged after the squawking bird, pinning the injured wing against her body. More squawks. The girl held it at arm's length.

Enclosed within the inner tube, the tern flung itself at the rubber walls. The dog barked and pulled at his chain. An older woman appeared; she and the girl conferred and she produced a peach basket from inside the camper. Then the girl unfastened the dog, holding him tightly by the collar and dragged him to the water; the animal was reluctant to retrieve the stick she threw until he was allowed to stand with both paws on her shoulders. To Tessa, they appeared to be discussing the rules of the game. Once or twice the dog lost interest and looked back longingly towards the camper. Gus wouldn't be left out. He made a great show of wrestling the stick from the dog's mouth, running into the water with energetic whoops to distract him. Charlotte approached the girl and pointed towards the dunes.

"Snitch," Tessa said to herself.

The bird had thrown itself out of the basket and was making its way towards the nesting grounds, the flopping wing leaving a telltale, sorry trail in the sand. The girl returned, the bird was recaptured, and the peach basket moved into the shade.

"What does it drink? Sea water?" Charlotte embraced the dog in an attempt to keep him still. Tessa thought they made an appropriate audience for her father's lecture.

"Probably," Gus said. "Albatrosses have a gland in their noses that distills the salt from the water. Maybe terns and gulls have the same thing." He sounded oddly tentative.

"I do know there are dissimilarities," he went on. "Terns don't care much to swim. It might be a least tern; they're somewhat rare." The girl seemed impressed.

"Give it fresh water," he decided.

The object of the discussion made no move. It was evident to Tessa that the bird had given up its struggle.

"Fish, that's what's needed." Gus thought of their dead bait, but the car was a long way off. Charlotte abruptly abandoned the dog and began to run towards the jetty, pumping her arms and lowering her head with each leap, blissfully ignorant of how graceless she appeared on land. She pried mussels from the lower, wetter rocks, scrambling up to drop them from a height the way she had seen the gulls do, and gathered the meat in a large clam shell. Running back with her prize, she laid it among some seaweed.

"Kik-kik-kik," said the bird.

"Let's give him time to get used to his new surroundings." The older woman invited them inside the camper, offering coffee she had cooked on a propane stove. She wore a sweatshirt over a bathing suit. Close-cropped gray hair. Muscular legs. Not her father's type at all, Tessa concluded.

"A nice way to spend a vacation. On the beach," her father said, being polite.

The camper was snug and complete. "We live this way much of the time." The woman, who told them her name was Lillian, took a bottle of brandy from a cupboard and poured some into two cups.

After she had satisfied her curiosity about how these people lived, Charlotte went back outside. Tessa thought someone should stay.

"The rest of the year we live in a house trailer," Lillian said. "Ever since my husband died. Not so much to take care of that way. Gives you the feeling you've got a certain amount of mobility even if the truth is you're firmly anchored in place."

The nomadic life looked appealing. Tessa forgot that she and Charlotte could not peacefully share a bedroom larger than this entire camper.

"I admit, sometimes Rosemary and I get in each other's hair. But it's a matter of choosing the right companion," and here Tessa saw the woman look hard at her father. "I mean, that's essential when the space you're working with is so small. Of course, we don't always have a choice, do we? I've been lucky. Rosemary, she's really not my daughter. She came to me the year after Frank died. That was my husband. Before then, it would have been out of the question."

Tessa remembered Edward and the other strays her mother had taken in and forced upon them. A neighbor's son lived with them now; his parents had moved and he was finishing out the year until he graduated from high school.

"Likewise with the dog," Lillian continued. "We picked him up at the animal shelter. I think that accounts for why we get along so well. It's easier, somehow, with strangers. I personally think it has to do with members of one family having the same chemistry. It's a wonder how some relatives can bring out the worst in you."

This notion appealed to Tessa. All her problems with her parents and sister could be as simple as chemistry. Too much of the same. And the garage barely able to contain all of them in summer.

"What does a woman alone need with a big place? It was Frank's house from a previous marriage. He hadn't finished it; sometimes I think that's what drove out his first wife. He was still working on it the day he died. 'Lillian,' that's all Frank said. His final word. He seldom called me that. Had a whole string of names, not all Christian. There was something else in his voice, too, like he'd been caught with his pants down."

It was obvious to Gus that he wasn't going to get any more to drink; he drained his cup.

"I found him sprawled half in and half out of the space under the house where he'd been trying to get at some pipes. All I could think of was that he wasn't a baby and I mustn't be too gentle with him. I worked on Frank's chest. Can't think if I remembered to pinch his nostrils shut. The neighbor, a nurse, she found me pounding away. She swears I was muttering something about the fire extinguisher. We had one, you know, for an emergency. Well, this was an emergency, wasn't it? The knowledge of that extinguisher close at hand was somehow reassuring to me. Funny what goes through your mind at a time like that. She didn't have any more success than I did and she was a professional."

"We really should see after the bird," Gus said, getting up to leave.

"Do you know what someone advised me to do at the funeral after I told them of my decision to sell the house? Take calcium. As if Frank's death had leached all the starch out of my bones."

Lillian had hit her stride and there was no stopping her. Maybe, Tessa thought, she had been into the brandy earlier, but that was not evident in the way the woman moved expertly about the camper, sidestepping the sporting gear strewn about, ducking her head where the ceiling jogged to drop over the sink; she began modest preparations for their meal. Rosemary came inside to get the dog food and water. From the way the girl handled herself, it was clear the pair were perfectly capable of taking care of themselves. Tessa's mother and aunts were too, but somehow the women in her family didn't seem to realize this.

"Do you miss him?" Gus was annoyed at his daughter's question, not wishing to prolong the conversation.

"It's amazing what you can learn when you have to. Things I couldn't imagine myself doing while Frank was alive. Besides, at our age," and here she winked at Gus, "we're allowed a bit of foolishness, right?" Tessa could see this really annoyed her father, who believed he was younger than everyone.

"What will happen to the bird?"

"Don't worry, these things have a way of taking care of themselves," Lillian reassured her.

"We could go into town and buy it some tuna fish," Tessa suggested to her father, but he was done with their little adventure.

Maybe they were wrong to try to save it. Tessa was sure, as they walked through the dunes, taking a different route to avoid the nesting birds, that the tern wouldn't eat the mussels, would die because it was being prevented from making its way home. Just as well. If the bird lived, it couldn't fly; it would be tormented by curious beachgoers, its fate similar to the skate's.

She looked back at the camper. Lillian was hanging up wet towels on a line strung over the peach basket. With each pinning, she nudged the basket along with her foot. Over her shoulder, in the water, the dog was paddling furiously, neck outstretched to keep his head above the breaking waves, valiently trying to keep up with Rosemary, who struck out with purposeful strokes toward the horizon.

When they reached the inlet side, a jeep was parked next to their car. A fisherman was bent over his pole, intent on baiting the hook. Gus greeted him with questions about his catch. "How many? What kind?"

A nod towards his bucket indicated they would find the answers there. Silently and patiently, with his back to them, he reeled in and then cast out again, unlike Gus, who fished by setting his pole in a holder in the sand and waited for a strike. With each flick of the man's wrist, the line transcribed a falling arc through the air, pausing just long enough for them to admire the stringent image before it touched the surface of the water and sank.

Gus drove the car slowly, avoiding the potholes.

"We'll never live in a place like that," Tessa said, pointing to a house in the shape of a hexagon.

Her father said they wouldn't care to. "All those rich people have problems." Unlike Frank, he would finish his house, and, once completed, it would suit them. The rectangular design was simple and functional, the masonry able to withstand any hurricane.

A motorcycle pulled out of the drive. It hung on their tail awhile, which made Gus slow down even more. Passing, the cyclist raised a fist. Tessa waved back.

Their father decided not to go home just yet. He stopped off at the White Horse Tavern. He bought the girls 7-Ups with ice and straws, beer for himself. They played a little shuffleboard. The sand itched between their toes and inside their underwear; they all needed a shower. But Gus was trying to keep the afternoon going a little longer. After all, there was no hurry, no fish, nothing, to spoil.

15

After serious deliberation and last-minute revisions, the three were dressed, Lottie wearing a light blue cardigan with the mother-of-pearl buttons running down the back, Sabine looking like a churchgoer in her best navy dress and short gloves.

"Take off the hat," Tessa said. She herself had tried to strike a practical medium, choosing the comfort of low shoes and a full skirt, although one made of silk.

Charlotte had given up accompanying them on these expeditions about the time she gave up all control of the family checkbook to her husband. This saddened her mother, but Tessa could do without her sister's view of them as spendthrifts.

Lottie set the pace, taking long strides, and Sabine hobbled along in her faille skirt trying to keep up, Tessa bringing up the rear; the sidewalk was only wide enough for two. When they got to Laurel Hill Boulevard, Sabine insisted on stepping off the curb first, holding her daughter back with her arm until she deemed it safe to proceed.

They struggled up the hill past the Gothic replica whose much-admired tower had been transported brick-by-brick from England, the house's flower beds now hemmed in by five identical concrete stacks. If Sabine was distressed over her sister's gardenless existence, she had only sorrow for the tenants of the Projects, deprived of light and air. Deeper sorrow, still, for the veterans of the last world war who flew past them in their wheelchairs, racing to beat out each other and the advancing rain. They deftly negotiated the traffic islands in their commute to the reconverted Bulova Watch Factory, where they toiled in the service of peacetime luxury.

Lottie and Sabine negotiated the metal steps to the elevated on tiptoe, so as not to catch their heels in the grating. It was midmorning and the three women had no trouble getting space together in the empty subway car, their knees touching, the backs of their stockings shredded by the wicker seats. Instinctively they leaned into the turn as the train rounded the curve entering Queens Plaza, relieved once again that it had not hurtled off its tracks and tumbled them onto the sidewalk below in front of Tavar's Bridal Salon. Tessa looked at the people in the ads, smoking cigarettes while perched on the decks of small sailboats, and yearned for blue water. Her mother whispered something to Lottie, who grabbed her sister's arm as she raised it to point.

Sabine appeared to become more visibly agitated as the train crossed the river and began its descent underground. At each stop, people got on who seemed to have no destination in mind except to ride the loop, their outfits assembled with no purpose other than to cover and warm themselves. A policeman cradled a helmet in his lap as if he had lost a horse or a motorcycle.

At their stop, they were pushed off and swept along through the underground arcade. Sabine halted in front of a florist's stall. Tessa dragged her away; she feared it would only bring up memories of a similar passageway on 34th Street-- a conduit for the railroad commuters--and her mother's own flower-selling days in the shop of a man named Alex. Sabine would say that everything since then had been a mistake, and where would that leave her daughter?

They exited one by one, pushing at the metal bar of the revolving gate and hurried into daylight. A man lounged on the subway steps, basking in the drafts of warm, exhausted air. While her sister and niece pretended not to notice, Lottie hung back, and peered into his face, reassured by the lack of recognition.

Their destination was 14th Street where Klein's department store occupied an entire block on Union Square. The labels had been cut out of the clothes; only the meticulous seams and linings distinguished those of the major designers from the inferior merchandise. It was rumored that some of the wealthiest women in New York shopped there.

Tessa waited for the moment when she spied something that made her breath quicken, gold shining among the dross; she grabbed before someone else did because, although she could live without it, she didn't wish to. Only a few times had she resisted temptation; the ones that got away still haunted her. She had brocade jackets too formal to wear with anything she owned, and shoes whose fabrics changed color although they were lying in the back of her closet where no light reached them.

Sabine looked around critically at the handful of customers, taking her measure of the early arrivals, those most in earnest. She headed for the dresses first, where they always started; separates in a place like this were likely to be scattered and you could get a headache trying to reunite them. Tessa always checked the label remnants, Lottie the seams, and Sabine the tag. When Tessa held up a dress she was seriously considering, her mother asked, "What's the original price?" If the difference was great enough, she would tell her daughter to buy it regardless of whether the color or style was flattering. Color was important to Lottie, who took items to the window for a better look by natural light. You had to be patient to sort through the rows, the dresses squeezed together on the poles so tightly you chafed your hands getting at them. You had to have a practiced eye to sift out the good stuff. You had to not need anything too badly. Sabine and Tessa started from opposite ends of the rack, holding up dresses each thought the other might like. Sabine piled garments onto her daughter's arms, which were already burdened with her jacket; they always dressed too warmly.

Then she moved on to the tables, lifting, examining, Sabine's discards snatched up quickly by someone else; a gray-haired woman in a suede suit obviously considered this her territory.

"Your mother could learn a thing or two from that woman," Lottie whispered to Tessa, picking up a sweater and idly rubbing the material between her fingers. "Do you think it's cashmere or lamb's wool?"

"Let me see that," the gray-haired woman asked, and Lottie handed over the sweater, much to Sabine's amazement. She would never have given it up so easily.

"Don't you have enough?" Tessa complained, her limbs aching under Sabine's selections.

"Find us a dressing room," her mother said. "In all of this, there must be something that fits."

Not necessarily. Often the sizes were cut out along with the labels; standing in front of the mirror and pulling the dress over the one she was wearing, Sabine tried to make an educated guess. What did it matter, her daughter thought; she was going to take it all anyway. And she would urge them to do the same. Something too large for Lottie might fit Sabine or Charlotte, but Tessa was taller than any of them.

"We can always let out the hem," Sabine said, holding it up. "Or take in the waist. Twenty-percent off, another ten at the register. How can you lose?"

Inside the dressing room, women of all shapes were standing on piles of garments, naked but for their slips. Tessa much preferred taking the clothes home before trying them on, enjoying the anticipation of how they would transform her appearance, her life. The dressing room was all reality, misshapen bodies; even Lottie's thighs flared out from the tops of her stockings. Someday I will look like that, Tessa thought. Childbirth had nothing to do with it. She was being confronted by her heredity. Once Tessa had come upon her mother in her room pulling up her panties. Everything was there to see: the body of a fifty-year-old woman, active, a gardener and lifter of heavy bundles--laundry and groceries--but none of that activity seemed to have translated itself to her slack muscles. Everything was loose, hidden by the folds of clothing. Tessa found the furthest corner from those two, but her mother would rather she stand guard next to her loot. Do up the buttons Sabine couldn't reach. Why bother to try anything on? They had a seven-day grace period. It could all be returned next week.

At the checkout, the counter piled high with her culled treasure, Sabine covetously eyed a scarf of soft green mohair, and held her breath as the woman ahead of her in line debated about its purchase.

Outside, they crushed the bags, expelling the air, and smashed the items together.

"We'll straighten out everything later," Sabine said.

Usually she and Tessa grabbed an Orange Julius and a frankfurter at the Nedick's stand, but this day the three went into the Woolworth's and sat at the counter. Over their tunafish sandwiches and tea they peered inside the bags between their legs and tried to rekindle their enthusiasm for the items long enough to carry them home.

Lottie was sorry she still hadn't found anything for Rudy; she liked to dress him to please herself, then stand him up in front of the relatives and show him off. Sabine never bought anything for Gus. Each week tools or building materials, sometimes plants arrived on the stoop, purchased with a portion of the paycheck that never made it home so that his wife wasn't clear how much money he made.

They cruised the windows of the shops around Union Square, those with awnings to protect them from the rain. Tessa paused in front of the Ansonia store admiring the suede heels, their rhinestone buckles catching the light. When her mother insisted, "You have so many shoes already," Tessa marched inside. They had an eight-and-a-half narrow. She convinced herself the heels would go well with the sequined bolero jacket, an outfit suitable for an imagined New Year's Eve when that holiday wouldn't be celebrated with her relatives.

Lottie said little, but admired the shoes. "I wonder if they would have them in my size," a compliment to her niece's taste. "I guess it wouldn't do for us both to be seen in the same pair."

"A different set of clips would change the look entirely," Tessa pointed out. Lottie declined again, more firmly, and Tessa knew her aunt was just backing her up; Lottie's shoes were all imported, the leathers from South America. She preferred slingbacks and open toes.

Next to the shoe store in a men's clothing shop where very little was ever on sale, Lottie found a wallet she liked for Rudy. Sabine nudged her sister, trying to get her aside while the salesman explained that it was made of eelskin.

"We could go back to Klein's where they'd have it for half the price," but both Lottie and Tessa knew that Klein's didn't carry that sort of item. The salesman wrapped it up as a gift.

Lottie said, "You have to pay other places for that service. The wallet is worth it. Rudy will have it for a long time; he kept his last one for eight years."

"You don't need to go on," Tessa said, "to justify the expense," annoyed at the paucity of her arguments. Irritated that she was, once again, getting angry with her mother, as she inevitably did when they shopped together, for forcing her, and now Lottie, to agonize over each purchase. Did she really want it? Or did she merely wish to show that she was independent of Sabine's opinion. Tessa worried she might be one of those people who was afraid to pay full price for anything.

"Save it for Rudy's birthday," her mother said, as they walked towards the subway.

"The point of a present is to be a surprise," Lottie said. Tessa thought, if I was my aunt's daughter, we would be living in the poorhouse, but there would be compensations.

Her mother countered, "What did he ever do for you that you should be so generous?"

Lottie stopped. "Sabine, remember, he's sick," her tone

suggesting her sister should be ashamed to insult someone who was slowly killing himself by drink. Tessa wondered why it was that after all this time and all the two had been through together, a man could still come between them.

A vendor had set up shop at the entrance to the subway and was selling umbrellas. Sabine held up a black folding model with a plastic handle. Lottie opened another with an elegant wooden knob at the end. There were tropical fish, realistically depicted in the manner of a nature print, swimming on a cream ground. And a gilt tip that looked as if it was never meant to strike pavement. The umbrella was too long to be collapsible, it was the kind you were always getting poked with on the subway. It was spectacular. Tessa thought the fact of its singular existence among the other umbrellas was something of a miracle. Lottie had to have it. There was a marked difference in price, of course, and the vendor, sensing he had already cinched the deal, wouldn't bargain.

"The color's too light. The rain will stain it the first time it's used," Sabine said. The look on Lottie's face told her sister she had better not go on. Wronged into silence, Sabine turned away as if she was about to cry.

Tessa knew that her mother didn't understand what it meant to reach out for something that made your heart ache. The only catch was that you had to be able to afford not to have to compromise. Her daughter also knew it wasn't entirely Sabine's fault. Tessa wondered if it had been a tossup between the umbrella or buying Rudy the wallet, which Lottie would choose. Clearly, her mother thought it should be neither.

Sabine did take some satisfaction in the fact that the man gave Lottie no bag to wrap the umbrella in and that, shortly afterwards, the snap to close it was found to be missing.

. . .

There were few seats on the train; it was the beginning of the rush hour. It would be a tight squeeze, but they could all sit together. Tessa stood and the sisters created a little space, a buffer, between them. The train swayed and her mother's head began to nod, but she shook herself awake before it touched Lottie's shoulder. Lottie patted her sister's knee as if to aid her dreams.

At Queens Plaza they climbed the steps to the IRT, up into the humid air and the doughy smell emitted from the Nabisco factory. The neon sign on the roof of the Sobo Glue plant burned pink in the dark sky. Tessa was instantly reminded of her childhood fears of those pitiable horses sacrificed to the Sobo family trade.

The three women were shoved inside the car and separated, wedged tight against strangers as the train threw them into the curve. Reunited on the platform at their stop, Tessa saw the bus down below and ran ahead with the packages to warn the driver they were coming, Lottie and her mother clutching each other and the railing, struggling to keep up. The driver wearily indicated the giant clock face over the Bulova factory doors; he wasn't going anywhere for at least ten more minutes. Long enough for Sabine to step into Walt's Bakery. She came out with a fruit cake and Napoleons, announced they were both for that night's dessert, showing them she, too, could be extravagant. Then she hesitated.

"Well, maybe the Napoleons tomorrow."

On the bus, seeing how her mother leaned over the pastry boxes, shielding them against any sudden movement, Tessa felt her annoyance soften and nudged Sabine's foot; she wanted to protect her mother the way she had been protected from her father.

"Come and get me, please." Tessa called from in front of the darkened bakery after she had missed the bus again; it would be at least an hour before another. If, as she suspected, her father wished for his actions to be imbued with impor-tance and a certain heroism, now was his chance. He had to hear in her voice how she needed him. In his she heard a hesitation, a possible reluctance. He was slow in comprehend-ing. Every Tuesday and Thursday she had late classes. He had gotten this call before. He had fallen asleep in his chair. With luck, her mother would be apprised of the situation and force him to come.

Tessa had to allow time for her father to rouse himself, splash water on his face, cream his hands, change into warmer clothing, find his shoes, coat, hat, and cane. Allow for the long, painful walk of her rescue. He was often slower than she anticipated and she more impatient. Tessa stayed as long as she dared inside the phone booth, pulling on the handle to keep the door shut, but that made a beacon of the light over her head. Then, not wishing to linger on the dark, deserted streets, she ran most of the way, past vacant lots with bushes tall enough to hide a rapist. She scarcely saw another person; no woman would be out alone at that time of night. If a man did appear, Tessa ran faster, swinging her bag of books but straining to hear if he followed close behind. Approaching the Laurel Hill overpass, she slowed, breathed deeply, getting her second wind, knowing that once she had started, there was no turning back. The high walls made it impossible to see if anyone lurked there. Laurel Hill Boulevard was within two blocks of her home. Conceivably, if she screamed loud enough, her father would hear. Sometimes Tessa saw him just as he reached the corner. Then she slowed to a walk. Never once did he have to cross the Boulevard.

When she reached the other side, Tessa mumbled, "thanks" and kept going, anticipating his annoyance at having been awakened to so little purpose. Since she had started attending college, they didn't speak much to one another, not even in anger, her father already afraid his daughter knew more than he did.

"I can't walk so fast," he would say, trying to keep up.

Tessa ran up the front steps. He had left the door of the house unlocked as if he wasn't going far; anyone could have entered while her mother was there alone. She swore she had to manage this by herself.

"On Thursday I'll try to make the bus," Tessa said. On Thursday, she called again.

When they were let off, it was still raining.

"Time to christen the umbrella," Lottie said, but Sabine looked as if she thought it would be advisable to wait for a more opportune time.

"Maybe when the rain isn't coming down so hard..." Grudgingly, she huddled beneath the constellation of fish. There was room only for two; Tessa's silk skirt would be ruined.

Lottie said she couldn't stay for dinner, just a cup of tea, she had to see about Rudy, then sank into the down sofa cushions. Tessa brought the tea to her there, but she declined the cake. Sabine was disappointed that Lottie would miss the best part, the opening up of the packages and the decisionmaking, which was easier if several people were involved.

"How will I know what to keep and what to return?"

"All of it," Lottie sighed, not being much help, then struggled into her coat. The label inside was old, but impressive. Tessa thought how nice to be a person who didn't waver, who so clearly saw how much things were worth.

They watched Lottie take the shortcut to the bus past the incineration plant; the City hadn't bothered to put in sidewalks and the unpaved road was littered with glass. Maybe that was why she walked so uncertainly. At this time of evening, the buses ran less often. Her shoes would be wet by the time she reached home.

Sabine tied on her apron because Gus would arrive soon and the potatoes took a long time to cook. Tessa went upstairs to her room, the morning's rejects--sweaters and blouses--still on the bed where she had flung them, and closed the door. She slipped into the shoes, fastened the clips and pulled on one of the brocade jackets. In the face of such extravagance, she had better marshall her arguments. Without her aunt's presence, surely she would have to convince her mother, again, of their practicality.

Sabine yelled up the stairs, "If you don't wear those shoes outside, you can still return them."

Rudy phoned. Would Cat be home soon? The call had nothing to do with her uncle wanting his dinner. "Is it still raining? Maybe I'll go down and see if I can catch her getting off the bus."

At least, Tessa thought, Lottie had the umbrella. "She seemed tired."

"In that case, I'll take the car." His niece knew he wasn't supposed to drive; his wife would probably be glad to see him anyway.

"Lottie's bought you a present," Tessa blurted out. She couldn't help it; she wanted to make things right.

"Oh, good." Rudy didn't sound in the least surprised.

"Something useful." She didn't think it was the gift he most wanted. "And beautiful," Tessa added.

He laughed as if such a thing were not possible.

16

Mrs. Klemmer rummaged among the roses. She salvaged only the fullblown, those on the verge of collapse, and plunged them into the crystal vase on the table. Lottie brushed the petals from her plate. How pleasant, she thought, to labor in a garden where so little exertion and equipment--a straw hat, gloves and scissors--produced such a lush result. Mrs. Klemmer removed the gloves when she poured the coffee for her guest. Lottie reached for another merengue, this one in the shape of a swan, and surreptitiously licked her fingers.

The Klemmer house was located on the outskirts of Munich proper, beyond the last stop of the bus line, set at the edge of a small, parklike woods. They had come out on a Sunday, the cake balanced on Lottie's knees, the gift-wrapped bottle wedged between Rudy's feet. Their bags had already been deposited in a hotel near the train station; they could no longer presume they would be invited to stay. Since their visit was unexpected, they had walked the additional mile to the house, unsure of the welcome they would receive. Their relationship to the Klemmers was a remote one, a tenuous connection through Rudy's brother-in-law. No one had answered the bell when they rang, although Lottie could hear scurrying noises inside.

"We thought you were Jehovah's Witnesses," Inga Klemmer had laughed.

Mr. Klemmer was as congenial, if not quite as open in manner, as his wife. He came home in the middle of the day.

An attentive lunch was followed by a serious nap; upon awa-
kening, he returned to his office. In the evening, after a light
supper, he donned leather shorts and a hat with a feather in
the band and went hunting in the nearby woods. Rudy, who
hesitated even to fish, declined August's invitation to go along;
he said he'd spent enough time outdoors with his work.

The signs of the hunter's skill were everywhere. Towels
hung over soft paws in the bathroom, hats and scarves were
draped on antlers in the hall. A doe's head stared at the key-
board of the piano while Marta, the Klemmers' daughter, practiced. These were the smallest deer Lottie had ever seen, inha-
bitants of a fairy wood; they couldn't have run very fast, no
match for August's legs, sinewy and powerful in their shorts.

On Saturdays, all the members of the household, male
and female, visited the "friseur" and then, freshly coiffed, nails
buffed, walked arm-in-arm through a forest preserve. Here
lambs drank from baby bottles offered by children and a
miniature train carried them past wolves in cages. From his
seat, Marta's fiancé howled in poor imitation, scattering the
peafowl who strutted along the tracks, until Marta begged him
to stop. Peter was several years older, in his last year at the
University. Lottie had never seen anyone that young, so self
assured. Rudy, perhaps recognizing a landsman, judged Peter
would come to no good.

"Every pot gets its lid," Inga said, giving her daughter's
shoulder a squeeze.

Marta was sensible and sweet, with a settled air that Lottie
admired. The girl extended her fingers so that they all might
get a better look at the antique ring from Peter's family, set
with a modest stone. Instinctively, Lottie looked down at her
own hand, the pale outline of her wedding band still visible on
her finger. It had taken a jeweler's saw to remove it. She had

gotten less than she anticipated because, as it turned out, the stones were flawed.

August Klemmer, unarmed and restless, kept a large buck in his sights. His wife urged him towards the distractions of the beergarden and lunch, but not before he had promised Lottie a set of antlers for her very own. Two bottles of home-made wine were already in her suitcase, a parting gift from her brother-in-law, Gus', relatives.

The detour to the remote village had been a mistake. The family now owned only a few vines and the grapes were sold elsewhere for pressing. Gus' nephew, Dieter, commuted on his motorbike to the electronics factory in the next town when he wasn't helping on the farm. A discotheque had been built in the center of the unpaved square, an unsuccessful attempt to hold the young people closer to the land. Little else had changed. After seeing the toothless smile on the face of Dieter's father, who still lived in the stone house where no screens kept the flies out, Lottie understood the young man's frustrations. She could empathize with Dieter's mother, unhappy at having been left behind when the others fled to America and avoided the barn where Enna had strung herself up. Lottie did pay a visit to the "schloss," the manor house once owned by the wealthiest family in the village; Gus had their coat of arms duplicated on a set of drinking glasses. Now the fachwerke was crumbling and a pig rooted around in the courtyard under a line where clothing was hung out to dry. In deference to her brother-in-law's memories, Lottie had taken no pictures.

In Munich, the Klemmers installed Rudy and Lottie in their attic room which had a sink and toilet.

"Just like Sabine's house," Lottie said, and felt instantly

at home among the stored boxes of holiday decorations and outmoded clothing. While Rudy shaved, she made tea on the hotplate, keeping an eye on the suitcase with the bottles tucked inside.

The couple could stand upright only in the center of the room, where the rafters came to a peak; Lottie spent so much time bent over, she began to complain about her back. She had to strain her neck under the faucet to wash her hair; Rudy helped rinse and then she washed his back with even, sure strokes, getting water on the floor. They dried each other vigorously with the towel, then tumbled onto the bed.

"Scratch my back until it hurts." Lottie was acquainted with every part of that mottled landscape. She knew what followed this ritual.

"More," Rudy said. "Lower." Already there were marks like the cross hatchings of a mad engraver. She looked down at her nails with their perfect ovals and decided she wouldn't give in to desire. She would, however, give herself up to compassion.

"How can you do that?" Sabine had asked, incredulous, when the two sisters compared the private details of their married lives.

"How can you not?" had been Lottie's reply. Perhaps, she thought, something had eluded them, a settling into normalcy that other couples, even Sabine and Gus, took for granted.

After awhile, Rudy sat up. "It's still the same for us, isn't it?"

Lottie had consoled herself; she could always be certain she and Rudy would be together, in or out of bed, and all the sacrifices had been made to insure that end. But now she couldn't say how it was between them; she wanted to tell Rudy it was all right, that the preamble, the hugging and kissing, had been the best part for her, had always been, even when he couldn't make his body do what he wanted it to. She was no longer sure of the lengths she would go. Lottie planted her feet on Rudy's warm back and concentrated on the exotic smell of the Klemmers' soap on her husband's familiar body, to which she had less and less access. It was like being in prison, putting her hand on the glass, barred from the touch of the beloved's fingers pressed against the other side.

"The same," she whispered.

They all went dancing, or rather, the young people danced and they watched. When Peter invited Lottie onto the floor, she had difficulty following his lead; he misinterpreted her hesitant steps as defeat and they quickly sat down. The night-club was small, and their knees were uncomfortably intimate under the table, meant only for two.

When she found out how much Lottie enjoyed singing, Marta bought them tickets for the opera. When Lottie pro-tested she had no appropriate gown to wear, Marta offered one of hers. The ankle-length garment came to Lottie's calves. She tucked the extra material at the waist under a belt; in someone else's clothing, she felt less like herself. At the last moment, they didn't attend because Rudy wasn't up to it; Lottie was sorry she didn't have the opportunity to show him off in his dress clothes.

Peter rowed them around the English Gardens; Lottie would have liked a turn at the oars, giving her some control of the situation, but her back hurt. And, she was uneasy; Rudy had gotten into the homemade wine. There would be no pleasure for her in this outing. Usually taciturn, Rudy was talkative, luring his prey, in this case, Peter, into his conversational web with social pleasantries. Later, in the café where he was sure to steer them, after a few more glasses of wine, her husband would become even more garrulous, then lose what little tact he possessed. Declaring his intention "only to be honest," Rudy would blurt out just those words calculated to bring forth an angry response. But it was Marta's pity Lottie dreaded most.

The lanterns on the prow of their boat attracted insects. Peter said something and Lottie laughed out of politeness; a moth flew into her mouth. She waved her arms and Peter took this as a signal she wished to go in. He began rowing for shore.

"My wife is very excitable," Rudy said, standing, broadly imitating her gestures.

"Sit down, please," Marta entreated.

Suddenly Rudy's arms flew up and outwards, knocking his hat into the water. In an effort to retrieve it, he fell out of the boat. In her surprise, Lottie swallowed.

She saw her husband try to gain his legs, lose his footing in the muck, slide down among the reeds. She felt like she was the one underwater, the one who couldn't breathe.

"Not to worry," Rudy said, "I have my feet pointed downstream."

Never had he appeared so graceless, so much the clown. Reluctantly, Lottie offered a hand; it would serve him right if they left him there.

"Get in, get in," Marta implored.

"It's so close to shore," Peter said, afraid they would capsize if Rudy tried to regain the boat, "he can walk out."

. . .

"This is the last time I take you anywhere," Lottie said angrily, rinsing the lake water from his shirt in the attic sink. Rudy took exception to her words.

"You take me no where," he said, trying to muster some dignity, because she made all the arrangements, paid for everything. It had been several years since she had gone to sea as a ship's cook; she'd had to abandon that temporary refuge. No longer could she leave Rudy for any length of time. He would have been just as content to stay home, he told her; she knew he could drink anywhere. But she needed these holidays, happy for a time to pretend there was an existence beyond the watching and worrying, the cleaning up. And, in recent years, she had chosen to visit her homeland over more unexplored regions. Maybe she was becoming more comfortable among her own people. Or timid. Lottie knew it would have been twice as hard with him someplace else, to explain, smooth things over, in another language.

Rudy sat in the garden, reading the paper. Nearby, Mrs. Klemmer, armed with her shears, culled and snipped. Since he diligently refused all offers of coffee or sweets, she was free to go about her tidying and found him no trouble. Sometimes Rudy walked in the woods. Sometimes he retreated to the attic room and drank; then Inga steered clear of the third floor. Lottie went to the museum.

Peter sat not far away from her on a bench in the garden of the Alte Pinochotek, predicting from which aperture of the statuary the water would next flow.

"That's no feat," Lottie said. "You spend far too much time here when you should be in classes."

He said he wanted to practice his English; he wanted to come to America one day. Peter spoke eloquently to her of the

Dürers in the museum, the subject of his present study, how the painter lifted a commonplace fragment out of the ordinary and placed it in the realm of magic.

"It's almost religious." She almost wished to believe him.

Peter mugged in front of Franz Hals' laughing portraits and Lottie envied him the openness of his desires, his conviction they would be satisfied. So unlike Dieter, she thought, his ambition constricted by responsibility. Peter led her by the hand from picture to picture. She longed to rub his wrist back and forth with her thumb, but refrained from acting on the impulse; Lottie saw her husband sitting on a chair in the middle of their attic room, ill and unshaven, his knees drawn up to his chest, while she bathed him with a wet cloth.

"It's a long way down," Peter said, as they climbed the narrow church steps. "Better not to look."

The openings between the risers gave way to empty space; if Lottie's heel caught, she would be pitched forward into nothingness.

"Take your shoes off," Peter commanded, and she did. He turned in the narrow passageway to reassure her.

"Give me your hand," he said. She chose instead to grab hold of his belt loops. Lottie half walked, was half dragged, up to the top of the steeple.

"See, isn't this worth it?" Her face was flushed. She wanted to sit down, but there was really no place, so she leaned against the rail and looked out over the rooftops across to the Rathaus. She wished Rudy had come; he would have loved being up so high. But that was a different man.

"In which direction do the Klemmers live?" Peter leaned in to point. "No, in English," she demanded.

"You can make it out, among the trees, just beyond the twin spires of the Frauenkirche."

"And shall we go there, too?"

"Do you wish to attend mass," he responded irritably, she thought, "or do you ask merely as a tourist?"

"As a tourist," she mumbled, suddenly ashamed. She felt a lack of mystery in her life, the future a spiritual uncertainty. But he himself had urged her up these steps; they had bypassed the altar and the statues of the saints in favor of the view. Lottie turned and leveled her eyes at him.

"Now comes the hard part," she said. "You have to get me down again."

The Klemmers were going to Lake Constance with friends; the outing had been planned long ago, so nothing could be changed. Marta made herself a new wardrobe for the occasion, refusing Lottie's offer to help with the sewing.

Peter telephoned ahead. When he arrived, there wasn't room for the suitcases and all of them in the Klemmers' car, so he stood in the drive flapping his handkerchief. Mr. Klemmer drove like someone possessed, on the highway barring any car from merging into his lane. At the train station, Mrs. Klemmer, looking embarrassed, stammered some words of sympathy, alluding to Lottie's marital burden. She apologized again for their abrupt departure, then produced a small silver spoon with the crest of the city on the handle. Lottie realized she had bought no presents, not even something for Marta's engagement, nothing in exchange for the antlers now bundled in her dresses in the suitcase.

Rudy and Lottie settled into their compartment, which they appeared to have all to themselves. Wearily, Lottie put her feet up on the bag too heavy to lift onto the rack. They heard banging at the window.

"What is your address? Your address," Peter shouted, his face appearing and disappearing at the glass as the train began to move. "Maybe I will come to see you."

Rudy scribbled their phone number onto the train schedule and threw it out the window. Well, they wouldn't be home for awhile and maybe the beauty of Lake Constance and Marta in her new clothes would make him forget his plans.

At the next stop, a family took all the remaining seats and started preparations for the evening meal. They offered sausage and wine, but Lottie declined, feeling nauseous. Rudy refused only the food.

Traveling north, Lottie was drawn to the lives she saw reflected in the windows of the shops, restaurants and houses; eagerly she scanned the faces on the platforms.

Seeing her fixed attention on the landscape, Rudy accused his wife, "You're sitting on this train dreaming of some other, more interesting place," when, in reality, she sought glimpses of home.

A cousin had settled in the Ruhr Valley after the war. Caspar had his share of problems and had found nothing to distract him from their contemplation. Still, Lottie felt, that didn't excuse his unenthusiastic welcome. She and Sabine had sent packages: coffee, tea, cocoa, clothing with years left of use in it. They were taken to a restaurant on top of the television station, the most expensive in the city, and Lottie paid. She liked Caspar's wife. The woman filled the tub with hot, perfumed water and then pushed her fingers through Lottie's hair while it was still wet so that it dried in soft waves. So much pleasanter than straining her neck under the faucets on trains or in the Klemmers' attic.

Caspar tried to convince Lottie that it wasn't politically wise to venture into the East Zone; his name was on a list of defectors. She took this warning as a challenge, and decided to go to East Berlin, to visit her friends, two sisters widowed by the war. With meat purchased from the best butcher in West Berlin hidden under their coats, the couple walked across the border, Lottie confident that her married name was sufficient cover. But when she and Rudy handed over their passports for inspection, she suffered several nervous moments, then spent weeks trying to make up to her friends for the fact that at home she had a car and a refrigerator with a freezer. That her clothing was not ridiculously out of date. That she had a husband.

The visitors quickly saw all there was to see in the old city. The restoration of the buildings destroyed in the war was going listlessly forward, their modern replacements dishearteningly ugly. At the Pergamon, the statues were inside, protected from further contamination by the toxic air. These were not the remnants of a glorious civilization; Lottie looked upon the truncated limbs and headless torsos as ancient wounded. During the day she and Rudy took their own chances in the open air, breathing shallowly, and strolled on Unter den Linden.

Unaware of the correct procedure, and with little influence or connections, there were no tickets to be had for the Staatsoper. There were no flowers on the table, and no fancy cakes, but the women proudly served their guests stringbeans, which were considered a delicacy, on what was left of the family Meissen. Lottie coaxed Rudy into letting the younger of the two give him a haircut since he had staunchly refused all along to visit the friseur.

Travel was a reward Lottie believed she owed herself for something suffered or lost in her life. East Berlin felt like a punishment; they stayed as long as they dared, to atone for their freedom to travel and to visit friends and relatives at will. Rudy stayed sober, so as to feel the full brunt of what he believed to have been his previous defection.

At the airport, the U.S. Immigration people didn't want to let him back into the country, something about Rudy's papers not being in order, which frightened his wife. Lottie begged to accompany him as he was led away to another room, but they said that was unnecessary since no translator was required. As she waited, hoping Rudy would hold his tongue already loosened by several drinks on the plane, Lottie made a promise: if returned to her, never again would she let her husband out of her sight.

17

Lottie died first, herbal teas, leeching, and the crunching of bones having had little prolonging effect. No amount of stroking did any good; Rudy climbed onto the hospital bed and tried to rub life into his wife's limbs while the nurse restrained him. Lottie's circulation had always been poor; on cold nights he had covered her feet with his own so she could sleep.

The family had long been prepared for Rudy to go first, having seen his jaundiced body in a VA hospital bed more than once. Lottie's demise was sudden; the reasons for it were still unclear. Somewhere between the doctor and Rudy an important fact was lost in the translation. There were obvious gaps in the family medical history for which, someday, Sabine suspected, her children would pay. The unexplained deaths were the hardest for her; she wanted to know what they were heir to.

"Why was the cut so small?" she asked, remembering the long, raised scar on Gus' chest where they had taken out a lung.

Her daughter's husband suggested they get a lawyer but Gus was set against that idea. All of their lives whenever they got into serious difficulty--something hard work and determination couldn't counter--a lawyer had intervened and escalated their troubles.

Sabine always feared her sister would be burned to death, Lottie's flannel nightgown having once caught fire when she leaned over the gas burner. She fell off a ladder, making an already bad situation worse. The doctors informed Sabine that all the tests proved negative and that Lottie could go home for Christmas. On Christmas Eve, they decided to operate. The nurse would have insisted she take off the earrings before surgery even if it was only to make a show of cutting and sewing her up again. There was so little room in a hospital for style, but Lottie would have managed it.

"You're signing your life away," Sabine said, when they brought the consent form.

Although Lottie died quickly, she took a long time getting buried; Rudy wouldn't sign his wife's body out of the hospital. Hans was called, but was unable to reason with his brother-in-law. He sat, and wrote in a cursive more reflective of Lottie's slant than his own, "Be patient with him. Rudy will come around."

After the forms were filed, there was a gravediggers' strike. When Lottie was finally interred, it was in a cemetery where the cars rushed by on the highway, their speed unchecked by the broken paving. The grave markers were metal squares set in unmown grass. Perhaps, Sabine thought, she should have been buried at sea. All Lottie's friends were in Norway, South America or Europe and were unable to attend. A few words were spoken, a far simpler ceremony than that accompanying the burial of a pet rabbit.

Oscar's body had been laid out in a pine box made by Gus and put in the trunk of the car. The family piled into the pink Nash Rambler. Lottie drove, pulling the wheel first one way and then the other, compensating for a tendency the Nash had to pull to the right. She drove all the time now because Rudy's license had been taken away after the accident out West.

"Your half of the Studebaker, the rear end, is still good, right where I left it," he told Lottie. Thirty stitches had been sewn into his handsome head. A scar ran down the center of the forehead, swerving to meet the arch of his right brow; not even the blunt lock of hair combed down in front could conceal it.

They were headed for the Blue Ridge Mountains. It was winter and only Lottie seemed unconcerned as the car's nose pointed towards the ice-laden Delaware River, unafraid even of the trailer trucks which made the Rambler shudder as they swept past; she just gripped the wheel harder.

She did hit a squirrel. Sabine sat next to her daughters in the back seat, covering her eyes. The trip only confirmed the wisdom of her decision, although one forced upon her by her husband, not to take up driving.

At the farm, they shoveled the frozen ground in turns over the box, comforted by the fact that only old age had done Oscar in. That rabbit was fearless, chasing the neighbors' dogs for exercise; no other pets had survived life in the garage among Gus' turpentine pots. He lived on a diet of wild clover and chocolate wafers. After Oscar had eaten his fill, Lottie swung the animal over her shoulder. While he tried to get a toehold in her stomach, she vigorously patted its back. Sabine thought that was how it was when people had no children of their own.

After a great show of parading old Army rifles, a three-gun salute was fired across the grave. The site was marked by a tree stump on which a brass plaque engraved with Oscar's name had been nailed. The "boys" chopped off the heads of some chickens on another stump.

"They're going to expect us to eat them." Charlotte made a face. The birds danced around for awhile, the blood falling on the snow.

They said no prayers, for Oscar or for Lottie, at least audible ones. They didn't make a show of religion in that family. In fact, most of the women had married outside of their faith, married Catholics. Almost all, lapsed. Lottie was no exception.

"The proper way to greet a nun," Rudy once told his nieces, "is to place your thumb on your nose and wiggle your fingers."

When they looked confused, he said, "You'd better get your licks in while you can," as if he'd had experience in the matter.

After Lottie's death, Rudy's descent was rapid. Sabine did what she could, catching the bus under the elevated almost every day, walking up the three flights of stairs to the Brooklyn apartment.

"I always took a deep breath before stepping inside," she said, "because I didn't want to rely too much on that air," peppered as it was with the ashes of hundreds of dead cigarettes.

She flung open the windows. Rudy confined himself to an overstuffed chair, newspapers and a thermos of Lottie's herbal tea laced with bourbon beside him on the floor.

"It's a wonder he doesn't set himself on fire," Sabine reported. The wooden faces of wizened men carved in the Black Forest, bottle stoppers, leered from their lineup on the sink.

She helped Rudy out of his clothes and into the bath,

tried to persuade him to make for the bed instead of the chair, then, losing that battle, settled him in with a cup of soup on a tray iridescent with the wings of tropical moths. The stuffed alligator, which Lottie had insisted was Brazilian in origin, had fallen down from the wall above the bed where it had been crawling and was resting on the pillow.

The suitcases plastered with stickers from 50 years of travel were standing by the door ready for Lottie to make a fast getaway. Her last wish had been to see Alaska, especially the polar bears, a far cry from the tarantulas lurking among the bananas in the holds of freighters returning from South America. When Lottie ran away to sea as a cook, there were rumors of a sea captain and returned affections. Sabine never judged her sister. When this man came to town with topaz earrings for Lottie and a bottle for her husband, Sabine gladly joined them both--Rudy begged off--for swordfish dinners at the best seafood restaurant in New York and the show at Radio City Music Hall.

In recent years, Lottie's travels had been curtailed as Rudy became more of an embarrassment. The couple visited friends and relatives in Europe every summer, then only relatives when the friends wouldn't have them. Later, she couldn't chance taking Rudy out of the country, but couldn't leave him home alone either. After the trips came to an end, Lottie stayed through the years of drinking when the outlines of their civilized life began to blur and it became harder to convince herself she led a charmed life.

Sabine hid the bottles, replacing them with juice. Rudy had his sources.

"But near the end, he didn't touch a thing. He must have

starved to death. I found him on the floor," she said, as if the unexpected effort of rising to his feet to take the paper in had killed him.

"The mail was lying near his head, piling up under the slot."

Sabine's daughter was not convinced that the final surge of adrenaline, or the liquor, had proven too much for her uncle's system.

"Rudy died because he was deprived of what he needed most. And that was Lottie."

Her mother gave Tessa a look of disgust. "Nonsense," she said. "A mind couldn't do that to a body." If she admitted it, they were all in trouble.

The police became involved in Rudy's death, making what should have been a family matter, public. And Sabine wasn't prepared, even after all those years, for her husband's reaction. Gus was no longer drinking, having retired and made his peace with the world; his family wondered at the ease with which he managed to stop. Now that he had time, he was spending less of it tending to the garden and more browsing through the flower catalogs, planning for future expansion, placing orders. The most exotic plants didn't survive in their climate but others he cross pollinated, hoping that way to achieve some kind of fame. Coming home from the police station, Sabine pushed away a recent delivery, a gingko tree blocking the front door, and sat down, eager for some comfort.

Gus looked up from his ordering and complained, "Do you know how many flower arrangements we've bought lately?"

And then Rudy, in Sabine's words, "drove the final nail into the coffin." In his will, he left most of Lottie's things, and some of her mother's, to his niece who never came around, except to put on a teary spectacle at the funeral. Sabine tried to make sense of it all, but this last deprivation only added to her bewilderment at losing both a sister and brother in one year, Hans having died six months after Lottie from complications of adult diabetes.

Sabine's losses were piling up. There wasn't anyone left to take care of anymore. Her children were well fed, decently clothed and housed. Of the other needs, she didn't want to hear. She was just discovering that she had a few herself. Being the survivor was no fun, especially when you couldn't drive.

She buried the only people she could talk to, feeding their odd appetites before they passed away, walking to the next town to get pigeons for the soup her mother craved and then couldn't eat.

All the deathbeds coalesced into one. Sabine sat beside, not on, the bed. She listened, not averting her eyes from the pale face. Her words sounded ordinary, with no special power to soothe; she patted an arm, a hand. At these times, and only then, was she an optimist, refusing to address the prognosis, making herself deliberately ignorant of it. She saw her mother's wounds that never healed, but didn't question the doctor. Not even when he pronounced, with certainty, that in the morning after treatment, her mother would be dead. Sabine took heart knowing that when the time came, she wouldn't have to sit by and watch her husband die. Not one to make promises, Gus swore he would never be bedridden; of that much she could be certain.

18

Distracted by grief, Sabine discovered, belatedly, that some family heirlooms--her mother's silver vanity set and good porcelain--were carted off by Rudy's niece from the apartment. Sabine was still bitter about this and wouldn't lay it to rest. It was not, she was sure, what Lottie would have wished.

Other things did come to them: A rosewood table, the legs tipped in maroon paint, a reminder of Lottie's slapdash attempt to cover the walls of the apartment with Gus' castoff colors, those once in fashion in the homes to which she used to be invited. Linen tablecloths, heavy with embroidery, requiring a strong pressing arm and great quantities of spray starch. A scratchy record of Lottie singing, approximating the original, undulating performance. Tessa wondered if it pained her aunt never to have realized that particular ambition, but then, some people had a knack for living that was inclusive enough to embrace all endeavors, however flawed.

Tessa took possession of her aunt's hair, twisted into a bun which she sometimes pinned to the nape of her own neck. It felt substantial, nestled there like a silky growth. She had never been seized by the desire to undo the plait, imagining that when Lottie grew tired of it, she simply lopped the chignon off in one piece.

From her uncle, Rudy, she had very little. Sabine quickly packed up the camel hair overcoat and felt hat and donated them to the Salvation Army, but not before retrieving the message in the hatband written in her sister's hand, admonishing him to stay inside. Rudy had taken to doing his drinking out of the apartment while Lottie was in the hospital and she feared he would never make it back home safely; all the doors were identical in the attached buildings which went on for several blocks and it was a wonder he found his own. Lottie put notes in her husband's hat the way other women tacked messages to the refrigerator door where Sabine thought he would be more likely to see them as he reached for a beer. But he drank whiskey then, neat, no water or ice.

Tessa rescued the army blanket, a relic from Rudy's days in a conscientious objectors' camp, and the Smith Corona on which she had her first typing lesson. Unlike her mother, she felt she had received a handsome inheritance and hated herself for the times she had been ashamed, not only of Rudy and his drinking, but of Lottie. While vacationing together on Cape Cod, Tessa had chopped off her long hair to look like the college students she saw on the beach, those freed of vanity to pursue loftier subjects, but freedom proved elusive sitting on the same army blanket with her mother, sister, and aunt. Lottie exposed her round white belly to the sun. When she swam, it was with an exaggerated overhand gesture, a thwarted Australian crawl, her head up so she wouldn't get her curls wet. At the movies in the little theatre in North Truro, she laughed loudly. It was like being trapped next to someone singing all the wrong notes in church and fearing people would think you were the offender. Sabine laughed as if she was clearing her throat, apologizing for momentarily finding the world amusing, but so low only her daughter heard.

Tessa and her husband had been planning to have Rudy and Lottie over for Christmas dinner to see how their place turned out; her aunt and uncle had helped them move into an old four-story house in New Jersey, Lottie showing up for work in her fur coat and hat. Kneeling on the kitchen floor, she had attacked the old linoleum with a plasterer's knife, the cushion of plump skin on her knee puffed out of the torn stocking. Rudy washed the windows, inside and out, including those on the top floor. It was a long time since he had been up so high; the element of danger was great, especially if you weren't sober. Tessa felt she owed both of them her gratitude. She felt she owed Lottie an apology.

Maybe her praise of Rudy's efforts was a bit effusive. After all, he did have to pry the windows open after they had been painted shut for many years. But Lottie's exertions had been equally heroic. It was just a way the women in Tessa's family had--with the exception of her aunt--of bending backwards to please a man while all the time vilifying him behind his back.

The linens, rosewood table, and typewriter were packed up. There was hardly time to look back on tragic events; Tessa's husband was transferred to Washington State and the New Jersey house with its refurbished kitchen floor and shiny windows sold quickly. She hadn't wanted to own a house since; renting was like always having your bags packed, Tessa reasoned, remembering Rudy's advice couched in terms of his own portable profession. Besides, if you kept moving, there was no time to indulge in nostalgia. But regret was another matter. The secret was not to confuse the two, a trick she had yet to master. She moved fast so what her family had wouldn't be catching. When Tessa found herself working in one job too long, settling in, she moved on to another; no one was going to accuse her of becoming a specialist. She wouldn't give up or give in, not like her mother did to her father's obses-sive, demanding ways, not like Rudy to his disappointments, however gracefully, nor like her other uncles, resigned to lives of diminished opportunity. She had an option which neither her mother nor Lottie dared possess. For Tessa, the word "divorce" was a hidden weapon to be unsheathed and brandished at any moment on the unsuspecting, on the husband and children. On the mother.

Sabine called to find out how they were all faring. She inquired after Tessa's husband. Informed that he was in the garage, or still at work putting in overtime, she would demand to speak to him, afraid he had gone missing.

She was fond of her son-in-law. After all, he was a good provider. He neither smoked nor drank except for an occasional glass of red wine. He wore unfashionable attire, making him appear older and more serious than he was: an old black raincoat, the pockets stuffed with gloves, his pants pulled out of line by the weight of the jackknife and nail clippers. Tessa thought it was a kind of victory for her father that she had married a man who also wore his pants unstylishly low on his hips.

Once Lottie had introduced her niece to an elegant Norwegian, soon to be a captain of his own freighter. They all went away for a weekend to the Blue Ridge Mountains where some of Lottie's fondest memories were invested.

Rudy disparaged these as foothills. "You should see the Rockies."

"I have, remember?" Lottie said, and edged away from her husband on the front seat, gripping the steering wheel at its base, retracting her elbows so as not to touch him even accidentally. Willing him to be on his best behavior.

The four did some cave exploring. The Norwegian was diffident, acknowledging the much younger person that Tessa was, helping her over the rocks. He lingered in the Chapel of the Bells, where marriage ceremonies were performed, interpreting for her the drippings from the roof in terms suggestive of images in clouds or dreams. But when he offered to massage the back of her neck in the car, Tessa ran as far and as fast away from that weekend--within the limits of politeness-- as she could. At the next rest stop, she changed seats.

One love replaced another; there was never room in a life for them all, or maybe just not room for the person you were when you felt that way. When Tessa was younger and so had much less to lose, she could afford to weave a fantasy around those she loved or rather, create the fantasy to better love them. Although she was no longer impressed with any feats her father pulled off in his later years, the man who cartwheeled down the beach and swam a quarter of a mile against the current each summer day had her begrudging, undying affection.

She distinctly remembered him taking her home from the movies on his shoulders, her eyes shut against the moths that flew against her face as they passed under the streetlamps. But Sabine insisted the movie theatre was a bus ride away and he never accompanied them. Tessa came to know that her father had started to go to the bars long before she grew into the questioning, irritating and judgmental adolescent she believed drove him there.

Her mother still harbored a resentment against her husband that was hovering just under the surface, ready to be dredged up after the second glass of wine. Why did Sabine wait until now to attempt a retelling of the story? She was a deaf old woman full of secrets and they were killing her. If she sat down to write, in whose hand would she pen her version? She was an unreliable witness. But neither was the past quite like her daughter made it out to be. Tessa only knew how she felt then, and that was real.

"Did my piano survive the trip?" Sabine had asked. Tessa worried that her father missed it. She, herself, didn't know how she would get along without one. With each piece she played, she entered new country. Her child turned the pages until she grew bored with their intimacy. Perhaps when she was older, they would tackle duets; while Tessa attempted a soft harmony, treading gingerly on the pedal so as not to drown her out, the girl would be assigned the melody. Tessa might even have to endure "Malagueña" again.

"And how are the children?"

The grandchildren were fine. They would always be fine even if they were not. It was a mercy not to burden her. The members of her family had a way of coming at the truth slant-wise, as if staring at it directly was not to be endured. Tessa knew who among them always painted the rosiest of pictures or, in her mother's case, found the worst light in which to view even the most innocuous of events. But even the staunch-est realists became rationalists in the face of a dire physician's report.

When Sabine started in on Rudy and how he ruined her sister's life, Tessa refused to hear it.

"You wouldn't feel that way if you had seen her. At the end. Seen him."

Tessa no longer could recall the color of her uncle's eyes; they were trapped in the creases of his face. She carefully, selectively remembered other things. It didn't hurt that the couple were handsome and childless and so showered their nieces with souvenirs from their trips abroad; because she was the oldest, the Japanese pearl in Charlotte's ring was twice as large and the gold links in her Florentine bracelet weightier. But Charlotte proved to be the one true compromiser in the family and, therefore, the only one destined for contentment; Lottie and Rudy lost interest in her.

One day, driving north on the highway, contemplating the further Alaskan north to which she was tempted to continue, Tessa passed a grey Studebaker, its belly dragging the ground. She half expected to see Lottie at the wheel, elbows working in response to the road's bumps and turnings. Instead there was a man in a soft, cotton hat, a tourist; the plates read not New York but Ohio. Besides, her aunt's car was long gone; it died somewhere in a ditch in Colorado. Tessa was fond of that old car. As a child, she would sit between her uncle's legs and steer while they ate cherries from a paper bag and spit the pits out of the window. She preferred to believe it was the very same Studebaker, resurrected by a junk dealer and towed further west.

Some day Tessa would sort out what was indisputable, verifiable fact and what the result of willful imagining. She knew it was a knack, to be worked at like a piece of music, over and over, until you got it right. But worth the effort. It was good to be sure of at least one thing in this life, some small packable truth you could take with you when you were on the lam.

19

Untended, the tools were showing signs of rust. A bit of oil would do the trick, but the garden needed his full attention if it was to come into its own this summer. Gus had gone straight home from work, skirting the tavern where someone was sure to ambush him with useless talk, ate his supper in haste and donned overalls without showering. If diligent, he could get in a good hour and a half, maybe two, before dark. Make up for lost time.

When he nudged open the gate, bells announced his arrival; in his neighbor's allotment, beyond the wire and rail fence, a goat perked up its ears.

"Go ahead, mister," Gus addressed the animal, "Enjoy yourself, eat any old damned thing you please."

The sun gathered itself for the late afternoon show, bleaching the petals of the Japanese plum tree that spilled onto the pale gravel, and etching the angular roof of the tool shed in strong relief. Gus undid the padlock on the building, took out saw, clippers and a spade.

The pruning of the lilacs would have to wait until fall. The apple tree had unfurled its leaves; in a week or so it would be in bloom. No question of spraying now and harming the bees. Later in the season, the tree would be hung with caterpillars, but he could still coax the dogwood along with benomyl for its week of glory. Diazinon, pyrethrins, and fungicides were on the shelf next to the tools. Codeine on the medicine chest shelf. The chemical didn't make him better, just lulled him into believing so, like the alcohol before he had been bullied into abandoning that particular ally.

The garden was as close to perfection as Gus could make it. Years before, it was his own body he had tried to perfect, the muscles kept firm with regular swimming and tennis, the skin on the hands supple--despite their daily immersion in turpentine--with the application of costly creams. He wore gloves to keep the dirt from getting under his nails and in the creases of his palms, long, to protect his wrists from scratches when binding up the roses. Purposeful strides ate up the pavement; his walk now was uneven, a ragged affair. He stopped frequently to catch his breath. Breathing wasn't second nature anymore but something he had to think about, reminding him that he wasn't whole. Still, he should be grateful. That's what the surgeon had said.

"We got it in time, before it spread. Lucky man."

Gus sprayed the roses with preventive medicine, sulfur; the dust got up into his nose and lungs, his one remaining lung. The taste of metal in his mouth, like the blood the first time. Boy, he really could go for a cigar about now; giving it up was like saying goodbye to an old friend. He struck a match on the post, cupped his hands around the flame, and inhaled. From now on, he thought, it was going to be a matter of giving up, one by one, old comforts. Bit by bit, giving himself up.

He nicked the bark of the camellia bush with the spade and saw no traces of green. He dug it up and reluctantly tossed it onto the compost pile. It came out easily, never having taken root, preferring a more sheltered environment. Through his long convalescence, the catalog promise of double blossoms with peppermint candy-like stripes were a treat he felt was slight compensation.

He removed the burlap sacks from around the roses; it was weeks since there had been any danger of frost. The bundle of sacks reminded him of Tessa and Charlotte snuggled under the lap robe Sabine had made by piecing together the skins of an old mink coat. Now the back seat of the car was empty on the drives to their country place, unless his wife was stretched out there, taking a nap.

He leaned against the shed. There was no place to sit; there had never been the need before. Behind the house he had placed a marble bench where once in awhile an inquisitive child would kneel, but Gus rarely took the time to contemplate the fish as they came to the surface of the pond to feed. His first chore after getting out of the hospital had been to remove the boards and the straw that covered the pond. He was glad to see the fingerlings and counted the old fantails who had made it through another winter. The fish with markings like a black kiss on its forehead, Tessa's favorite, wasn't among them. Not such a bad way to go, Gus thought, one day simply not showing up.

He turned over the ground with the spade, then raked it into neat rows to receive the seeds: radish, lettuce, kohlrabi and spinach. He set up poles to support the beans and the tomato plants. The rhubarb was a sure thing, the frilled leafy fan already a show against the bare soil. His children had always grown it along with an embarrassment of pumpkins, cucumbers and squash, at least sowing the seeds in the ground and picking a few before losing interest. Not one of them had the patience or vision to be a real gardener; their father despaired they would ever learn anything useful.

He dug up the lilies, the result of his own propagation efforts, choosing the largest bulbs to be transplanted around the house where they might more readily invite praise. This garden on city land was where all the real work went on. And where any gifts from the florist ended up until they proved themselves. Gus heeled in a small azalea, a souvenir from the hospital; most likely its flowers had been forced and it wasn't winter hardy. He washed out the birdbath and filled it, then because he could see Venus glimmering in the sky, gathered the tools, put the sprayer on its shelf, and closed the door of the shed.

The bells stirred as he hooked the gate. He put out his hands to still them, not wishing to intrude on the sliver of silence that came at the end of each clamorous day. In another hour, the milk trucks would commence their rumbling.

Gus took his time on the tentative walk back to the house, picking his way around potholes and broken glass. He contemplated a leisurely shower, easing sore muscles, washing away the day's work, but couldn't shake from his mind the image of his body slowly eroding under the steady stream of hot water.

20

So much sand everywhere, the grains slipping between the piles of 2x4's, evading Sabine's broom. She chased the elusive drift under the remnants of frayed parlor rugs which were meant to hide the drain in the floor and to cushion the severity of the concrete; she did what she could.

This making do--five years now since they had moved into the basement of the house--was not so very different from the life in the garage, first summers and then year round after Gus' early retirement. Like animals always seeking a dark burrow, Sabine thought, the two hunched over, Gus with arthritis and she with an angry sciatic nerve, as if the ceiling pressed down on their backs. What light there was came from a small window in the door at the base of the stairwell and the fluorescent tube over the washbasin. A plastic shower curtain, hung in deference to modesty, screened the bathroom. Patches of mold stained the walls. Their clothing, the linen on Gus' bed, all smelled of the proximity to the sea. A heavy door, usually propped open, led to another room, this one smaller and windowless. Its walls were reinforced with steel intended to withstand the force of a nuclear blast; it served now as a wine and root cellar.

Sabine had painted the kitchen cabinets, the walls and the dining chairs white--the color, in her mind, of cleanliness--the shrouds of canvas piled in the corner the room's only gay decoration. The paint splatters were traces of the bold pigments Gus was mixing in anticipation of their final move upstairs.

Gus drew the blueprints, taught himself framing and plumbing but, defeated by the wiring, had to call in an electrician. The finishing, right up his alley, was going slowly. He often woke with stiff joints and seldom ventured far from the property; the steep beach stairs aggravated his bad hip and he had almost given up fishing altogether. His sisters, who had also migrated from the city, drove over to pay their respects. Several times a week Hedwig's old Buick, dubbed by the children, "the Green Hornet," loomed outside the door. Refusing to be entertained in the basement, she sipped her coffee on the patio and briskly ticked off the number of chores she had performed that morning and those that awaited completion by the end of the week. Even on the beach, she was not content to recline on her towel, but prowled the sand, gathering stones and shells for her garden. How disappointed she must be to see how little is going on here, Sabine thought, as she lopped off the spent heads of the petunias in the window boxes. She would give all the relatives something to talk about. She had her own plans and a fistful of lists to accomplish them, but somehow kept getting sidetracked, putting a good face, and another coat of paint, on their makeshift existence.

Sabine did manage, with a little help from her daughter, to get herself upstairs. Tessa came with her family and, of course, they were not to stay in a motel. And the damp basement had been out of the question for the grandchildren. Proper beds were set up, the new stove and refrigerator wrestled into place. Gus sensed a conspiracy among the two women to move things along. But that had been months ago, their visitors come and gone, and the furniture still rested on the underlayment. At least Sabine could go off by herself to the master bedroom while her obstinate husband slept downstairs. It spared her the indignity of pretending to understand what he said. "You mumble," she complained, blaming her hearing loss on Gus' poor diction.

Sabine lit her new stove and put the kettle on, its ancient insides encrusted with minerals that lent their taste to the coffee. She closed the kitchen window for the night, straining to turn the crank. Although unfinished, already the house showed signs of wear; the metal frames sweated, powdering the sills with a black crumbly growth. From the refrigerator she took an apple and the milk carton, moving aside the baby food jars of pollen, each labeled in Gus' angular hand. He insisted she continue to cook downstairs where most of the food was kept in the ice-encrusted refrigerator with its defective gasket.

She carried the cup of tea and a plate to her bedroom. From the bottom dresser drawer she took a box of chocolate wafers hidden among the packages of unopened stockings, the velvet jewelry boxes bound in yellowing Christmas ribbon. It was an old habit, holding something back for herself; already her grandchildren knew where to find the cookies. She could never bite into one without thinking of Lottie and what a fool she had been over that rabbit. Above the bed, her sister contemplated the meager repast. The painter had given her an elongated nose, somewhat finer than the original, but the eyes were as Sabine remembered them. Lottie's hair was swept away from her face in the color and style she had worn in her youth.

"You would be as gray as I am now."

She felt certain her sister was apprised of her plans. Aloud, she said, "It was so much simpler when we lived in the city."

There she could walk to the store, take the bus or subway whenever she felt the need to get away. Here she was at the mercy of Gus' moods or the generosity of Hedwig, who had a habit of taking her hands off the wheel to make a point as she drove. Looking back at that life it seemed intricate to Sabine, like one of her cutwork tablecloths. Now they followed a simpler pattern, aligned with the seasons. When the bad weather closed in they listened to the radio and read all day, Gus studying his seed catalogs. This past winter had been especially severe and they ventured outside the basement only for brief forays to the post office, butcher or grocery stores. Three days of silence went by before Gus relented and helped his wife dig out the car so that she might shop for the children's Christmas presents.

As much as Sabine keenly felt the restrictions of these gloomy months, daylight barely penetrating the windows and then only for a brilliant, brief flareup in late afternoon, her heart sank at the thought of the coming spring and the garden cleanup. The raking of leaves, planting, then fertilizing. The constant weeding and watering. Last fall, just before it had gotten too cold to work outdoors, Gus replaced a gangplank of two narrow boards, their only previous access to the front door, with some brick steps. Now he was going on about a stucco wall, but its purpose eluded her. The phone calls had been made; the materials ordered. Sabine knew that in a few short months she would be expected to push the wheelbarrow with its burden of cement sacks and sand, while Gus leaned on his cane and directed her progress.

"Not this year." She gestured towards the portrait, raising the half-eaten apple like a fist.

. . .

When her cousin, Caspar, had written suggesting Sabine visit him that spring, she had agreed hastily, before she could change her mind.

"Don't expect me to subsidize your wanderings," Gus said, when she first tentatively brought up the subject. "I have all I can do to pay the bills to get this place finished."

She knew that was a lie. She often heard him boast to his sisters of his astute timing in the sale of their city house which had coincided neatly with a sharp upswing in the real estate market. Well, she didn't need his money. A little had come to her on Lottie and Hans' deaths. She had given some of that to Gus, not all of it, in the hopes he would use it to bring their home closer to completion. But her husband was ignorant of the stock dividends which had accumulated over the years in her sister's account to which her name had been joined. It was a tidy sum as the result of Mr. Stern's fiscal advice from beyond the grave, although the interest was lost because the bills were in the bottom dresser drawer, stuffed inside the fingers of her gloves.

The weather conspired against her, catching Sabine without an umbrella in a sudden cloudburst as she stepped from the train. She had taken the bus to the railroad station, the train to the subway, then made the long walk to her old neighborhood. Harold Bronfman was glad to have the chance to offer Sabine a dry refuge, to fill her in on who among their neighbors had died, and who had gone to live with their children, in Harold's mind, a fate worse than death.

"They're going to have to carry me out of this house in a box," he said.

Sabine thought it was tempting fate to speak of such

things, and felt her resolve slipping. She declined Harold's offer to stay overnight and hurried away, averting her eyes from the improvements next door: the statue of the Virgin's feet embedded in the edge of a cement pad that echoed the shape of their old pond, the grape vines on the trellis elbowing out the roses.

After inquiring about her visa and passport, Sabine had her picture taken, reassuring herself, "these things never come out well," then walked slowly, peering into the store windows. Even with the new permanent, she thought, "Who is that old crow?"

In front of a bank, two Asian women were evicted onto the sidewalk. They screamed something about a key to a safe deposit box and shoved one another, until the guard came out and hurried them along. A man took a picture of his wife sitting in a hansom cab clutching a bouquet of flowers. "Don't show so many teeth," he said. He counted out the bills for the driver, spreading each one carefully and straightening it with the edge of his hand. "Germans," Sabine thought. A woman approached her, swinging a large set of keys on a brass ring. She tapped each lamppost as if keeping inner count, pausing just long enough to gouge the hood of a parked car with one of the keys.

Sabine checked herself into a hotel, thinking she would take a nap before dinner; she found the city exhausting. It was a modest place, located blocks from the East River. Harold had convinced her that part of town was safe. His own niece had been found on the lower West side wandering about, her wallet and all identification gone, three days of the girl's life still unaccounted for.

The walls of the hotel were painted a soothing, nondescript color, the pictures were of rural landscapes, and choosing a television program didn't engage Sabine in a battle of wills. She hung out the "Do Not Disturb" sign; it seemed an invitation to enter. Two men banged on the door, mumbled something about repairs, and began to tear out the windows, part of the ongoing and fruitless effort to bring the hotel up to the New York City Building Code. Soot blew in and speckled the pillowcase and bedspread. The carpenters slapped two metal windows in place, throwing the wooden ones down onto the sidewalk below, and smeared brown putty at the corners of the sill. It took forty minutes. Stickers dotted the windows like so many flattened moths.

"We're going to do the entire front of the hotel in two days," one of the men boasted.

When they departed, she wedged a chair under the door knob. The plasterboard wall was thin and Sabine was aware of the comings and goings of the other occupants late into the night, the slamming of doors up and down the hall. She told herself that in Germany, among friends and relatives, she would feel more secure. The next morning she showered nervously; the crack in the tile floor had been hastily mended, the raised grout like something live underfoot.

Charlotte had asked her mother to stay with the children for a few days. Sabine had been unusually anxious, knowing all she had left to do at home before her trip and one night she was sure she heard someone trying the doors of her daughter's house. The dog barked and carried on, which upset the children and worried their grandmother. Charlotte came home a day later than expected and Sabine had been running to catch up ever since.

The suitcases were packed, lined up in the front hall. Her son-in-law was due soon to take her to the airport. She had heard Gus that morning, up at 5 a.m., boiling the water for his coffee. Not wishing to face him, she had tea in the kitchen upstairs; she would eat her breakfast on the plane.

"Gus?" Where could that man be? Looking out the back window, Sabine saw evidence that an ambitious project was in the works. The wheelbarrow, its sides caked with dried cement, was standing next to a load of rebar, which had been delivered in her absence. Gus shuffled up the driveway. Today he favored the cane heavily. It was one of those humid days that made his arthritis worse; she could almost taste the salt in the air. Impatient, Sabine gathered up her purse and raincoat. She wondered that she had come so far, without Lottie's encouragement. A car horn sounded. As she was going down the front steps, she noticed a hairline crack at the base of the new railing.

Gus was reassuring his son-in-law. "I'll be just fine. Now I can cook what I want to eat. It'll be steak and potatoes every night."

Sabine made a feeble attempt to hug him. He said nothing. Were they speaking this week? She couldn't remember. He looked at her with astonishingly bright eyes. He had never cried, not when the parakeet had flown off, not even when his daughters married and one had moved 3,000 miles away. Sabine told herself he was only feeling sorry for himself. Her leather bags laden with gifts were put in the trunk. They were much too heavy, she should have bought new ones, she would never be able to manage them alone. She climbed into the front seat. Gus bent over and leaned into the open window of the car as if about to impart directions. The vehicle was put in gear and inched forward.

"That silly fellow is going to get his toes run over," Sabine thought.

Her son-in-law had little to say. On the subject of Charlotte, he was especially silent, and resented any inquiries about his wife's eccentric behavior. Sabine knew if she asked him about his work, which was technical in nature, he would keep the conversation going until they reached their destination, leaving her free to contemplate her rash decision to abandon a sick old man. She found herself talking about her grandchildren, a more cheerful subject, but now she was leaving them without benefit of her protection. Especially Charlotte's littlest one.

The child had recently spent a few days with them, bringing along her pet gerbil. She would often take the animal from its cage, play with it, and then become distracted; forgotten, it narrowly escaped being sat or stepped upon. One day the gerbil went missing. They hunted upstairs and down, inside the root cellar and under the lumber. Gus said it must have ventured outside and taken up permanent residence with the chipmunks in the piles of rotting logs that dotted the property. This story didn't satisfy his granddaughter, who wouldn't be consoled with the promise of another pet.

The table was set in the dining room, a concession on Gus' part, telephone books propping up their small visitor in her seat. Halfway through the meal, they heard scratching from inside the newly plastered wall; Gus was especially proud of its smooth texture, his expertise with the trowel. The scraping went on for several days, the sounds at first urgent, then becoming progressively feeble. Followed by silence, except when they sat down to eat. Sabine tried not to think about it.

"A bird must be on the roof," she said, but clearly, the noise was coming from inside the dining room wall. The child wasn't fooled. She whined, pleaded. Cried.

"Gus," Sabine took him aside, "I can't stand it anymore. You've got to do something."

Surprisingly, he didn't give her an argument, as if he had already made up his mind. With a strength his wife no longer thought he possessed, Gus smashed in the wall with a sledge-hammer, cut through the lathe with a pair of wire snips, and freed the creature, which was frightened but alive, although barely.

"Now," Gus grumbled, pointing a finger at his grand-daughter, "make sure that thing stays in its cage."

Sabine had been more than happy to sweep up the debris, even though she knew months would go by before she would see the wall repaired.

At the airport, her son-in-law gave her a tepid kiss on each cheek and drove hurriedly off, late for work. Sabine rushed after the startled skycap to retrieve her bags. She located the limousine service and waited impatiently for the driver to fill the van with other passengers from incoming flights. By the time she reached home, it was almost dinnertime; she realized she hadn't eaten all day. She called her cousin in Germany, then a taxi.

Gus was sitting alone at a table by the bar window, a half-eaten sandwich on the plate in front of him. Sabine tapped on the glass; he didn't look up. She forced herself to go inside.

This wasn't the kind of place where husbands took their wives. The lighting was dim; the bar was not known for its food. A place for serious, solitary drinkers.

"Forget something?" Gus asked. He had the good sense not to appear smug. There was all that concrete yet to be mixed, the wall to run the entire length of the house, maybe a pillar or two.

Sabine unhooked his jacket from the chair. She nodded towards the waitress. "Pay the check. Let's go." Gus allowed himself to be helped up.

"I'll fix us something to eat at home," she said. "Steak. And potatoes. On the new stove. Upstairs."

21

Tessa and her mother were in the new kitchen, a room that Sabine was especially fond of, the rich honest cream of the plaster walls not yet vandalized by color. In between her quiet sniffling, she sipped coffee; her daughter drank a glass of milk. They were having a good talk. Sabine glanced apprehensively out the window to where her husband was cutting back the lily stalks, his head bowed as if ruminating over the dormant beauties.

Mother and daughter were both convinced that he was mad. It was the explanation they had come to, after all of these years and discussion. The other possibilities that suggested themselves were even more painful. But this conviction wasn't an easy one for Tessa; it carried its implications.

Gus admitted to a family "eccentricity" which, he said, manifested itself only in females. He was relatively safe in this pronouncement as he was the only surviving male on his side of the family, the rest having been killed in the wars.

His sister, Enna, had walked into the barn one day and hung herself. She was too young to have two small children, too young to be the only one left behind with a dottering father and an ailing farm when they all emigrated to America. The eldest sister tried to climb out of an upstairs bedroom window after all of her children had married, leaving no one to cook for. Aunt Hedwig had always behaved peculiarly, and Tessa learned early not to engage her in any meaningful conversation. There was something wrong with her logic; you could never be sure, when the talking was done, just where you would end up.

Tessa had a limited history. Sabine was introduced to her future husband by his mother, a strong-willed woman, already a widow. She, too, died before her granddaughter was born. Gus never mentioned his family and never went back home, but Tessa returned for him, and wept stupidly at the graves of people whose lives, she thought, had been impoverished by never having known her.

Her father said very little about the pictures his daughter took on her walk to the old stone quarry. Gus had etched his initials on the trees so many years before, the letters grown thick, swollen like his legs were now. He never mentioned the sandstone buildings in the next city--among them, the school that Einstein briefly attended--her paternal grandfather's mark prominently carved in the cornerstones. That the father's accomplishments were so much more public than the son's must have galled.

Tessa came to tell her parents about the divorce. Her father had phoned long distance after Sabine divulged her daughter's relationship with a younger man. Gus was pleased with his call, the first he had initiated in several years.

"I can't tell you how disappointed in you I am," he began, his tone suggesting that Tessa had finally revealed her true nature.

Gus had often promised that he would come and visit when things were better between them, but never could manage it. Sabine took home pink camellia blossoms as large as an open hand. She carefully measured their size with a ruler and informed her husband that they started opening before

Christmas and continued until May. Gus knew Tessa was no gardener; he had said so many times. He bought several camellia plants of the same variety but they didn't do as well on the East Coast. It never occurred to him that his daughter had little to do with their success; it was only by accident that she planted the bushes in front of the windows where they could absorb the heat radiating from the house. In fact, Tessa was embarrassed at the showiness of the flowers, their profusion and shockingly lush color; she much preferred the daintier, gardenia-like blossoms that turned prematurely brown.

At an age when very little was expected of her, least of all that Tessa show an interest in horticulture, her father had set aside a corner of their property beyond the reach of the shade cast by the evergreen trees. With a stick he scratched out a rectangle on the ground, defining the boundaries with a string linked by four stakes. Together they loosened the soil, Gus with a shovel, Tessa with a hoe whose unwieldy handle threatened to poke out her eye. The ashes fell from the cigar he had clamped between his teeth and they worked these in as well; later her mother would contribute coffee grounds and eggshells. Her father gave her a packet of seeds, petunias Tessa remembered, which she scattered indiscriminately. Later, with her help, Gus planted a tea rose and a clump of day lilies which he told her closed up at night because they, too, required eight hours of sleep. In spite of her neglect, never dividing the bulbs or fertilizing the rose bush, the flowers from these two plants graced their table summer after summer. If her father had intervened in their care, as his daughter came to suspect, he never mentioned it.

. . .

Gus laid the impending divorce off to his wife's side of the family, to aunt Lottie. He said his sister-in-law was a crazy, willful woman, and that his youngest daughter took after her. Tessa hoped so, especially now that she had the bump taken out of the middle of her nose.

Her father also took the opportunity of her visit to tell Tessa that he didn't approve of the way she was bringing up her children. He feared they would have no more respect for him than she did. His youngest grandson was happy to play in the sudsy basin of water while he shaved. It was only with adults that Gus lacked patience; they didn't think him wonderful enough. Already Tessa's oldest boy, at twelve, got restless when the stories of the Himalayan snow monster were repeated. He listened, but had long been a nonbeliever. He would have preferred to stay at home; no one paid attention to what he had to say and he had stories of his own to tell. At twelve, Tessa had loved her father enough to instigate their quarrels, to attempt to convince him that his view of the world was biased and narrow, while Charlotte sat at the dinner table covering her ears and Sabine complained of a knot in her stomach. Soon they could not eat together.

Gus and the boys were making smoke caves, digging in from one end, hollowing out the mounds of dirt that had been created when the foundation was poured. Tessa's daughter stood on top of one of the hills and poked with a sharp stick. Her mother was afraid that when the children finished their tunneling, one of them would fall through the roof onto the fire. Her role of dire anticipator was a tiring, but, Tessa was convinced, necessary one. If foreseen and the warning spoken of aloud, unexpected danger might be averted.

From outside came no shouts of alarm, no squeals of surprise, or pain. Inside, just the sounds of Sabine's soft crying and the hum of the refrigerator defrosting itself. Her mother had handled the major disappointments of her life quite well, although it was the small things that got her down. Sabine never forgot anything, carrying the old grievances, wounds, slights; this burden rounded her shoulders, making her appear shorter than she was.

Now Tessa placed a new one before her. Mother and daughter talked about their common battles, the years they had spent finding and redefining those lines from which they had to retreat, lines that seemed to exist only for them. Those conversations never started because they wouldn't wind up where they began. Silent meals, so there would be no upset stomachs or upset children. Her father had no idea where the lines were drawn and crossed over them many times, like a ghost.

He said he didn't understand why Charlotte was behaving so peculiarly after the birth of her last child. Why she had taken to collecting old chairs that were missing their seats or potting plants in bits of china all day long so that the dinners were served up cold and the dust balls and dog hairs swirled about the house. To which his wife responded, "You can ask me where she gets it?" For once, Gus had no answer. Tessa tried to make her mother understand that "it's them and us," but Sabine was looking at her daughter intently now, in light of the news she had brought her. She was unsure. Together they wondered on which side the grandchildren would fall.

Tessa watched her youngest son as he followed her father up and down the rows, his small head bent forward in rapt attention. Soon the boy would know when the bluejay came to take its bath and in which woodpile the chipmunks were living.

The two women were grateful for the momentary quiet, but Sabine was anxious and Tessa feared she was getting an ulcer.

Before leaving for the airport, they assembled in front of the half-finished stucco wall, Gus flanked by the children. Sabine assumed her position next to her husband. "Put your arms around one another," Tessa instructed from behind the camera, and her parents obliged, although uneasily. Then she took her mother's place, attempting to hug Gus' waist; her father didn't reciprocate, but reached down to touch his grand-daughter. She is also mine, Tessa thought, clasping the child's other hand, straining to complete the circle.

"What are you doing?" Tessa screamed at her father when the car began to slide, as if his control over the vehicle had been relinquished voluntarily. She was caught unawares, even though there had been premonitions, near misses. The State of New York had just passed a new traffic regulation and her father treated the "free right turn on red" as if it was a green light. His arthritis prevented him from looking over his shoulder. Gus asked his wife's advice before changing lanes, then, impatient, proceeded without waiting for a reply; Sabine's hearing wasn't so good. Besides, he had a Cadillac which he bought from one of his brothers-in-law, the kind of car only old men and teenagers drove, and he felt that its large body and fins rendered him impervious to injury.

They had been speeding, trying to make the flight. The children delayed breakfast, visiting the cave one last time, and hindered the packing up by misplacing their shoes, unsure they wanted to leave. Tessa had proposed that she drive, almost insisting; her father had been just as adamant and refused the offer.

After he had narrowly avoided hitting a tree and a fence, they came to a stop. Later, Tessa discovered she had blackened her eye, but no one else was hurt. The sequence of events was still unclear, just what it was that had propelled them sideways so violently. "Black ice," her father said, obviously shaken. He stared blankly at his hands on the wheel. His granddaughter gave him a consoling pat on the back of the head.

A yellow compact came down the road, hesitated, skipped, and spun once around before landing on the shoulder. Tessa and her mother looked at each other in astonishment, then shrugged, and wearily got out of the car. They walked back to where the yellow toy rested on the grass. There was no crunch of frost underfoot, no obviously wet pavement.

By the time they reached him, the driver was already unbuckled and had worked the door open. No, he wasn't injured, he was sure, at least he didn't think so, he said, testing his legs with a little dance. No, he didn't need any help, was glad he had been wearing a seat belt. Didn't care for a lift, thank you. Tessa would not have wanted to get back inside that erratic plaything whose mainspring seemed to have been wound too tightly.

"Shall we wait and see if it starts?" No, he wanted to be left alone, to puzzle out what had happened.

"Black ice," they said, with authority, and walked back to the Cadillac.

"What you can't see will get you every time," Sabine said.

Gus didn't inquire about the fate of the other driver; he said little of anything. The expression on his face, one of guilt, was new to the two women.

. . .

He had been grinning stupidly when he came home supported by the policemen. They treated him, and the incident, as a joke.

"As long as it's the first time," they said of his having hit a parked van and gone on his way, oblivious to the damage he had done.

Tessa and her fiancé were in her bedroom, hiding out from aunt Hedwig, who lived across the street and came whenever she saw the sportscar parked out front. They had missed the beginning of the late movie, decided to go anyway after Hedwig finally gave up and went home, were on their way out the door when the police arrived; too late to go back upstairs.

"You're always making a big deal out of nothing," her father said, turning to wave goodbye to his new, good friends.

Outside, on the stoop, the policeman remarked to Tessa, "Your father is a funny man."

There was no guilt over the women who lurked in the background during her childhood, women in bars, or "on the job." Her mother said she believed it never went very far with them except in her husband's imagination, but Sabine was never allowed to forget their existence. Tessa knew, instinctively, that they were no threat, her family secure in the bulwark of so many aunts and uncles. Once, Gus gave a lift to one of these women friends visiting relatives not far from their country home. Sabine had to suffer her heavily-perfumed presence in the car where she sat up front, and feign polite conversation.

Gus drove slowly to the airport. No one remarked as they passed the pileup of disabled vehicles, the van hung up crosswise on the divider, not even when they pulled over to make way for one, then another ambulance.

They said their goodbyes at the terminal doors; Gus was anxious to get out of the city. Tessa didn't thank him for bringing them safely to their destination.

"I never would have forgiven myself," he said, "if anything had happened to the children."

Tessa's silence did nothing to assuage his suspicion that he had been going too fast, that he should not have been at the wheel that morning. His daughter would never let him drive them anywhere again, and he knew this. Just as he knew she had been waiting for an excuse to forbid him.

"Don't, for heaven's sake, drive like a maniac going home."

Tessa watched her father walk away, limping slightly without his cane, saw her mother drape one solicitous arm over his shoulder. With the other, Sabine cradled Gus' elbow, steering him through the crush of oncoming passengers, like the dazed and unbalanced accident victim that he was.

22

"This is no time for vanity," Charlotte said. She was wearing a black dress bristling with lint and short, grey dog hairs.

Tessa's plane had been late, but she insisted on changing into her suit. She wanted to look good for the competition.

Only the immediate family was in attendance, although somewhat diminished: Gus' sisters, a few surviving husbands and their children who had never managed to get away. The cousins had pretty much grown into their destinies and were exaggerated versions of their parents, although, Margarete, singled out for her beautiful legs, still had them. Margarete's gaunt husband, rising to the spirit of the occasion, stared Tessa in the eye, and accused, "You've gotten taller."

They would always be those children who played together with abandon every summer, but never wished each other well. Set up, lied to, they didn't understand the rules: in spite of hurtful words, they were meant to love one another. The competition now extended to spouses and progeny: whose husband earned the most or came from the best family, who had the prettiest, brightest offspring.

They all cried, even Sabine, recalling a younger man who had been kind to small children and animals.

"What a kidder Unc was." Cousin Wolfie had grown bald and fat. He laughed about how Gus had put fiddler crabs in Frieda's bed, lifting the covers and emptying the jar of bait by her feet as she slept.

"I loved that man," Wolfie said, and Tessa believed him. "He always did exactly what he wanted." As if that was a courageous and moral way to live.

It wasn't, however, an attitude conducive to friendship. Her father's relationship with their neighbor, and his only friend, was made possible because Harold Bronfman was a guileless man. He appreciated Gus' lack of subtlety, that he always said just what came to mind, that he wasn't clever enough to be devious.

Harold didn't come to the funeral service; a misunderstanding about a joint sewer line had come between them. Tessa called Harold's daughter. Elaine had been her teacher in many things, especially in the cosmetic arts, the lavish application of eye makeup. In turn, Tessa ran her fingers up and down Elaine's arm; when she got over the habit of biting her nails, she was proud that the length could give her mentor a proper tickle. Elaine said she was sorry, but couldn't attend. It was nothing personal, but her life was in a state of flux; she just wasn't sure one day from the next where she would be. Tessa confided that her own marital path was strewn with a few rocks.

"Considering the miserable childhood you had," Elaine said, "what more could you expect?"

Tessa thought this remark, under the circumstances, indelicate. And a surprise. She remembered her earliest years, those in which Elaine figured prominently, as happy ones: roller skating at night, chasing waterbugs with sticks into manhole covers. Looking up to see the ash glowing in the dark from her father's cigar as he and Harold sat on the porch and complained to one other about their youngest disrespectful children.

. . .

A red carnation was stuck to Gus' lapel. Tessa plucked it off; he thought the flowers common. How could her sister not have known this about him? The coffin diminished the size of his shoulders, but the mane of hair was still full. She touched it, the coarse feel like that of the stiff boar brush he always insisted was best for his scalp. Her father had his good wool suit on. So did his daughter. Hers itched. It was hot on Long Island in September; it had been cool and raining when she packed. His blue-striped suit was inappropriate, Tessa thought, the old bathing trunks more emblematic of the man when he still had two lungs and could swim a mile to the State Park. Straight up went the arm in his Teutonic sidestroke, then down again, like a drowning man. While Charlotte mimicked her cousins by diving off the big rock, a sport strictly forbidden by the adults, Tessa waited anxiously until she saw her father walk slowly up the beach, spent. He always returned on foot, never swimming back with the favorable current.

Because he had been such a physical man, after that dirty trick was played on him, after they took out one lung, Gus succumbed to self pity.

"If it wasn't that the family needed me, I would give up."

Although Charlotte, Tessa and Sabine all were gainfully employed at that time, they left the hospital in a daze, feeling abandoned and frightened.

Gus never fully recovered. There followed an exaggeration of his worst traits, a lapse in taste. It was when the lamps in the shape of Roman soldiers were brought into the house and white carpet blanketed the wooden floors so they had to take off their shoes before entering. It was the time of the vintage

Cadillac used to chauffeur around the women with red hair.

This was the man Sabine had married because once, during a party when she had drunk too much and gotten sick, he helped her clean herself up. That was as good a reason as any, Tessa thought, for marrying someone. Her mother denied it. She still had difficulty sorting out the differences between sex and affection, love and kindness, losing track of just what it was she had expected.

"He was a good provider," the minister said. The eulogy, written by his sisters, did not include the words, "loving father," made no mention of his children, or grandchildren; Gus had been appropriated back into his side of the family.

"For a clergyman, that guy speaks too softly. I can't hear a word," Sabine complained.

After the wake, they went to a fast-food restaurant on the highway for their supper, a modest end to a modest occasion.

"If only he had gone into the nursery business," Tessa said, "all of our lives might have been different."

Her mother set her straight. "Don't you for one minute believe it."

The next day, as Hedwig drove them to the cemetery, she announced to her nieces that their father had been proud of them. Tessa looked at her in disbelief, then anger, this information having come secondhand and rather late.

"Why shouldn't he have been?" Her tone defensive. She thought of the misdemeanors of her cousins, of her aunt's own son, Wolfie. "What did we ever do that was so bad?"

Charlotte stared out of the window of the car in silence, but Tessa felt the censuring pressure of her sister's elbow against her side.

"It's been raining since the day he died. The sky wept.

See," Hedwig gestured expansively, "today, the sun comes out." Even dead, she believed her brother capable of influencing the weather.

The cemetery was on a hill with ancient elms and grave-stones dating from the 1600's. A man named Henry Hudson was buried there, the child, Tessa, convinced this was the explorer. She had set right the toppled stones, those her little arms managed to lift; there were a great many small ones. It was here that Sabine first told her daughter that her grand-mother had given birth to seven children, four stillborn. She and Lottie and Hans were treated like the miracles they were, with great care.

"My father never yelled at us. I never heard him speak a harsh word."

They were lucky to get a place in the old section of the cemetery because Gus never went to church; the feeling was they were edging out the Congregationalists who had a greater claim to the diminishing space. One headstone stood for Tessa's parents like the headboard of the double bed they had no longer shared, Gus preferring to sleep in the basement. Her mother's name and birthday were already engraved, waiting in suspense for the addition of the final date. Although she might wish to be buried in more loving company, with her own brother and sister, in this, as in much else, Sabine had little say.

Her new life was ushered in with a bang.

There was the problem of what to do with the stumps. Their carcasses punctuated the garden landscape, making it difficult to park the cars after the service. Another person might plant a fern at the base, or plunk a geranium on top.

Sabine hacked at the rotten wood with an ax, a futile exercise. A tractor couldn't maneuver close enough without knocking down the walls Gus had put up in a valiant effort to forestall the completion of his work, to stay alive.

Tessa and her mother cowered behind the car. Tessa's husband, sporting a hard hat, raised his arm ceremoniously, pausing for effect.

"He's like a kid with a big firecracker," she whispered, covering her ears. The arm dropped, the air vibrated, broken wood rained down on the hood of the Cadillac. "Pop must be bellowing in his grave."

When the remains had been pushed into a neat pile, Sabine ordered, "Take them out of here, I've been looking at those damn things long enough."

She saw how easily something so seemingly intractable could be moved by machine, recalling the endless runs with the wheelbarrow laden with dirt, sand and gravel. Tessa's husband said there was nothing you couldn't do with the right tools.

Greg set the mailbox out front so his mother-in-law wouldn't have to walk to the postoffice, and installed new locks on the front and back doors. He hooked up the used washing machine. Although hot water entered the tub when the "cold" button was pushed, and "warm" wasn't an option, Sabine wouldn't hear of it being changed. The spin cycle was nonexistent, made to order for a woman who preferred wringing out the clothes by hand. Tessa's pleas that her mother get a dryer fell on deaf ears.

"How do you expect me to get any exercise?" Sabine would continue to hang out the clothes on the line even in winter so that the towels were stiff as washboards; her husband's overalls stood alone as if inhabited. She had simmered his work clothes in a pail set on the burner, stirring them with a wooden spoon like a noxious stew.

Having done his part, Greg returned home, leaving his wife to ease Sabine through the first days of widowhood. Tessa reminded herself that it was the women on her father's side of the family, Gus' sisters, who had reacted strangely to the loss of those dependent on their care.

Tessa and her mother strolled in the garden. Sabine spoke wistfully of the new lilies that had debuted that summer, Gus' more successful experiments in cross pollinization. The flowers had been cut long ago, the notched stalks all that were left. One could only imagine their colors and shapes. Tessa took cues from the tags. Her father had named the plants after the women in his life: a brash yellow Hedwig, a shy white Enna, which still clung to its bamboo support, and a cluster of sturdy freckled Sabines. (Apparently, no Tessas or Charlottes had survived.)

Sabine nearly fell over a hose.

"Look down and watch where you're going. Wear your glasses," Tessa scolded, firmly gripping her mother's arm.

"Next year I'm going to spray the pear trees; the fruit all had worms in it. Your father never bothered."

"Hire someone. Don't do it yourself." Tessa flicked a dead rhododendron bud expertly between her thumb and forefinger.

Sabine pulled her arm away. "I'm not as helpless as you think," she said. "I chopped down the holly tree. Right after. I knew how he'd react if I tried that before. There were three: two males and a female. I wanted to make things even. Besides, it was overgrown and shaggy, the sharp leaves hell to pick up.

It was taking over. A few quick chops and the tree was down. Simple as that."

"Well, you won't get as many berries," Tessa said. This was not the response her mother had anticipated.

"The last time," Sabine continued, her face close to her daughter's, "I forced your father to go to the drugstore and get me medicine. I was very sick for a few days and I made him wear something all the time after that." With age, she was unburdening herself of all secrets. "Don't look so hurt. Your father drove me to it."

Tessa thought, we each, in our own way, manage revenge. She noticed that her mother's hair was now parted on the opposite side of her head. Why the style change after all these years?

Sabine was waiting for her daughter to reciprocate, share some complaint of abuse or neglect. A few years ago, Tessa would have said exactly what was on her mind. Did, in fact, reveal that she and her husband were having problems. Her father was never meant to know. Her mother had been quick then to point out that she, herself, in spite of greater provocation, stayed in her marriage. And, Tessa knew, it was not for lack of temptation.

The photograph was glued into the cracked leather album among their childhood pictures. Charlotte and Tessa stood in front of the window of a flower shop with roses in their hands. Alex's face was barely visible; he was inside among the shadows, peering darkly out through the glass. He had given the girls packets of crushed aspirin, to keep the roses fresh. Tessa had a pair of toilet-paper rolls suspended from a string around her neck, her binoculars. That day they had been to the Statue of Liberty because their mother said she wanted finally, and up close, to see what all the fuss was about. When questioned on the subject, Sabine would only say, "Riding around with Alex in the rumble seat of a car was one of the happiest times of my life." She talked idly about calling him up, but Tessa knew she never would.

"If I spoke, I bet he would listen. That man always had a courteous way about him," Sabine said. "Of course, we would have separate beds." She lowered her voice, "I can't talk about this in front of Charlotte; she thinks it's being disloyal."

This fantasy of the other man became somewhat confused in Sabine's mind; she was unclear just what she had confessed and what she had been careful to omit. She seemed to recall that the baker had a gentle voice, too. There being no photographic record, Kurt's name never came up unless it was as a casual aside to one of Tessa's reminiscences: "I'll never forget how Mr. Shea murdered those crabs." Or, "He never did put enough jelly in the doughnuts." Sabine found herself protesting in his defense; to even the most casual observer her pain was transparent, the passage of years having honed rather than dulled that particular shard of memory.

There was a storm. The lights flickered on and off, teasing like old times. The pump started, stalled and then kicked in again, but Tessa was no longer the child who, at the first clap of thunder, refused to stand near an open window, or run the water. Besides, this bed was made of wood.

Weekdays in summer, Gus and Charlotte worked in the city while Tessa and her mother were left to fend for themselves. It was a primitive rural existence, testing their endurance. On damp nights Sabine put hot bricks in their beds to warm the sheets. Water was carried some distance in pails; they set aside

a few gallons for those occasions when lightning struck the
pump house. Tessa climbed out of the metal bed and sat on
the floor while Sabine ripped the bobby pins from her hair.
Tessa was sure it was the lightning that would do her in. It
had entered through the open screen door, this time unan-
nounced by thunder, catching her unawares as she washed her
hair, hands immersed in a basin of water. It brushed against
her ear and then silenced the refrigerator with a loud crack. It
seemed to Tessa that her father was always getting them into
bad situations and then leaving.

Unable to sleep now, she thought it would be nice to have
a cup of warm cocoa laced with plenty of milk. Better yet,
to share a confidence with a sibling. A brother with whom to
take sides against the cousins. A son who might gladden his
father's heart and set a cement block without it cracking.

Once it was Charlotte she whispered to in the dark. Her
sister didn't say much, so Tessa felt her secrets were safe. They
played together in the cellar of their house in the city. Deeper
than a basement, closer to the earth, the space was inviting
to other creatures that hid in its warm corners. The boxes of
crocheted doilies and Christmas decorations, the books from
baronesses, were littered with the translucent skeletons of
insects. Behind these, the painting of Lottie, covered with a
sheet, eerily prescient, gathered its share of cobwebs. Charlotte
was less fond than Tessa of dressing and undressing paper
dolls, but tolerated the activity because she had few friends
her own age with which to play. She added layer upon layer of
inappropriate clothing--a tiara with raingear, boots with a ball
gown--until the cardboard figure gained another dimension.

When Charlotte was old enough to work, she and Gus

walked to the subway each day; Tessa often wondered what they found to talk about. Charlotte bought her sister presents with the first paychecks--a belt, or a piece of costume jewelry--until their tastes grew so far apart that the accessories became an embarrassment, and Tessa was never seen wearing them.

Charlotte began dating a man with a bearing and accent just like their father. She became like their father herself. Less generous. Judgmental. She told Tessa how to conduct her life. Charlotte had insights on practically every subject. Her qualifications seemed to rest in her new status as the object of someone's desire. Tessa didn't think her sister ever wanted, or imagined, anything more for herself. And having achieved this, she became jealous and guarded. More than once she warned, "Don't you try to come between me and my fiancé."

Tessa was floundering then, trying to grow up just as quickly, but not succeeding as well. She seemed to be one of the few people in her large and extended family who wasn't absolutely sure about everything. Shortly afterwards, Charlotte married and moved out, but Tessa considered herself the lucky one; after all, her sister still had to share her dresser, closet and bed.

Their old room was to be redecorated. Gus wanted to do something clever, but his daughter and wife, mindful of the failure of the gold leaf to adhere to the dining room walls, chose a simple blue-and-white paper. Hans came down from Scarsdale to hang it and Gus was noticeably absent the two days it took to finish the job. Tessa was sorry for her uncle, who felt he was the cause of this new tension, sorrier for her mother, who only wanted to make her daughter happy. But she reserved her greatest pity for her father whose expertise, once again, had been called into question.

. . .

Sabine was also having difficulty sleeping. Tessa heard scurrying, the sounds of a chair being knocked over. Her mother was pursuing something. The white cat again. She was at the front door; it was wide open, the chains dangling. Sabine pushed at the air with her hands.

"The devil. Now she won't go outside. Sometimes she jumps up onto my bed acting as if she wants to be let out in the worst way, then makes me chase her through the house. But I'm very careful; I realize no one would find me for days if I fell."

Tessa led her mother back to bed. "You're dreaming again," she said.

"Sit with me awhile." Sabine was in no hurry to sleep. "Right after your father died, I would hear the slamming of boards down in the basement. I knew it was him, finishing up. 'Come here,' I said. 'Let's discuss things.' You know your father was so careful with his appearance, keeping his weight down; you see how little good it did. I wondered if he missed creaming his hands, shaving, little things like that. I wanted to talk to him about it, ask him how he felt. I wasn't afraid, just curious, but when the noise continued for several nights, I said, 'Now, that's enough.' I was very definite. 'Go away; you had your chance to talk. Quit bothering me. I need my sleep.'"

"How brave you've become," Tessa said. In his earthly guise, the man could wither her mother into silence.

"Braver than the cat lady," Sabine responded, and they both laughed.

This neighbor, who was in her late 50's, retrieved frightened animals from the highest tree limbs. She dressed for her work in crampons and a leather helmet regardless of the weather; Tessa was sure a storm would never keep her on the ground. Before she began to climb, the woman would place her forehead against the trunk of the tree, as if communing with its spirit.

"I don't know why she does that," Sabine said.

"Maybe, mom, she did it once and it seemed to work and then it became a habit and she was afraid to stop. Like you're afraid if you quit waking in the middle of the night something bad will happen."

"Your sister tells me to get a dog; it would protect me, she says. Like as not, it would work the other way around; something else for me to take care of."

Tessa asked, "How do you think the dog would get along with the white cat?"

The walls of the bedroom in which Tessa was attempting to sleep had been combed for textural interest. The paint on the chair rail and moldings was applied in feathered strokes to resemble precious stone, but it had the opposite effect; when Tessa opened her eyes, she felt she was underwater. A slight tugging at the edge of the blanket woke her and she reached for it before it slid to the floor. The sheet had become undone, but she was too tired to get up and tuck it in. Then she must have fallen asleep again but only for a moment because the clock on the night stand had barely advanced when she glanced at it. Her shirt was hanging on a knob on the closet door, clearly visible. It seemed to be glowing. There must be a full moon but just as quickly Tessa realized this to be false. The light grew dimmer as if receding within the boundaries that defined the cloth, and she drew herself out of the confines of the blanket, stretching on top of the bedcovers to get a closer look without setting foot on the floor. Tessa stared in an effort to bring the features into focus: a dark man, with a full mustache, his hands grasped formally in front of him as if holding a bouquet.

"What do you want?" She thought the light grew brighter. Finally, in exasperation, Tessa said, "Go away, now that's enough," remembering her mother's boldness. "Do I have to repeat myself?" She tried to keep her eyes open as long as possible; it was her fixed gaze, she knew, that held the object to a recognizable shape, rendering it less fearful. Tessa thought hard about what words might make the apparition disappear, but wasn't sure she wished it to.

She awoke with a start to daylight, the sight of her shirt still hanging on the door, and the sound of something being dragged in the basement. The basement. Where her father had his last breakfast. The cup and saucer, plate and knife were still sitting on the table when her mother found him. He must have been trying to put on his shoes; he was bent over, Sabine said, partially clothed, sitting on the chair in front of the dressing table with the peeling veneer, his forehead swollen when the blood rushed to his head. At the funeral she was relieved to see that he looked more like himself.

"What are you doing?" Tessa yelled from the top of the steps.

"Eat," Sabine urged. "The muffins are in the broiler. I'm cleaning out."

Five toasters in working order, still in their original boxes, were stacked down in the basement, while upstairs her mother made toast in the oven.

"All right, I'll have breakfast, but then I'm coming to help.

Don't lift anything heavy." When she was gone, who would prevent her mother from doing these things? Sabine had spent a lifetime hunched over some bundle: groceries, sacks of cement, dead branches. There was no reason to believe she would stop now. Tessa walked across the kitchen to the light switch on the wall opposite the door, cursing her father for making everything, even the simple motion of turning on a light, difficult.

She marveled again as her mother bound up the old tool chest with rope. Sabine had strong hands, pulling upholstery fabric until it threatened to rip, then stretching tighter, an expert gauge of its elasticity. Her mother fashioned wreaths, bending the greens about the metal frames, proud of the fact that she never wore gloves.

In Alex's tiny flower shop, there was just enough room for the two of them. Located in the Arcade between 33rd and 34th streets, each rush of passengers on their way to or from the Long Island Railroad had sent their hopes soaring. Tessa imagined Alex, after an especially profitable day, pressing her mother against the ice box, his mustache tickling. "If I were to ask you to come down to City Hall with me, I wonder how you would answer?"

"I don't see why you want this old thing?" Sabine asked.

"I have so little from pop." The man didn't believe in presents.

Once a week, when the ice cream truck made its rounds, Tessa ignored the "No Riders" sign and hopped onto the running boards. She was deposited in front of her father where he was pruning the quince hedge planted to keep dogs and small children out of his garden. If she was in luck, he had some coins in his overalls which he passed over the gate as if making a gift to his daughter of the world; the dimes were always soiled.

When the cab pulled up, the driver looking severe and dangerous, Sabine made a great show of saying, "My husband will be home any minute now." The man had to struggle to get the wooden box into the trunk. Tessa paid extra to take it on the plane. It would probably fall apart, she thought; the nails and hinges were rusted from the salt air, the damp of the cellar held in the pores of the moldy wood.

At home, she delighted in her house, recently constructed, the smell of the raw, drying lumber; in this climate, there was no need for a basement. In the early morning hours while the rest of her family slept, she did the laundry. It was the sound of her son's overalls clanging in the dryer that made Tessa realize, once and for all, awake or dreaming, that never again would she see or speak to her father.

23

In her seventy-first, or was it seventy-second year, Sabine couldn't be sure--one day, one year seemed much like any oth-er--she found herself devoid of all responsibility and fresh out of excuses. With little practice and all the wrong luggage, worst of all, with no one to prod or nudge her, she set out in Lottie's wake.

Sabine slid, or rather was pushed, down the side of a mountain on a plastic garbage bag. It was unclear whether her screams were out of fear or delight that something could still surprise her in her old age. Tessa hadn't meant to shove so hard.

"God," she thought as the receding figure gathered speed, "if mom breaks something, she's going to be laid up in my house."

Sabine came to an abrupt halt against a mound of slush. Her grandchildren went by on plastic saucers; she was in danger of being run over. She was still struggling to catch her breath when Tessa helped her to her feet, brushing off the seat of the snow-caked ill-fitting jeans. As usual, Sabine had come unprepared; no sooner in the door, she asked to borrow some-thing: curlers, socks. It made her feel like they were chums. She missed her sister.

She had been lured out West by her daughter's promise of a trip to "Alaska," the word conjuring up images of eskimos and gold. Polar bears. Adventure.

The accommodations on the freighter weren't exactly as depicted in the brochure. The single cabin resembled the inside of a boiler room; foam insulation hung down from the pipes in the ceiling, hardened in mid drip.

On deck, Sabine's general prejudices didn't prevent her from chatting amiably with the Indian mothers and their children, so many, she thought, they must be Catholics, although they tried to convince her they weren't all from the same family, or even the same tribe. The youngest children looked down when Sabine spoke to them and she chose to interpret this as a sign of respect rather than shyness. When one of the babies refused to stop crying, she surprised it into stillness by throwing it across her knees and patting it decisively on the back. She hoped the women would wear their traditional dress at dinner, but no one seemed to change clothing for that meal, including the Hari Krishnas, who sat in their robes in a tight orange knot on the floor. Sabine persisted in her more formal attire, remembering other crossings, although the object now was certainly not to attract a man. The men on board, mostly construction workers, were a rough lot, but were careful of their speech when she was present, even asking her to sit in on a poker hand; solitaire and canasta were the only card games she knew.

Every Friday she and Gus played spirited hands of canasta with their neighbors, the Bronfmans. Sabine baked a fruit cake and Maria and Harold brought the wine. The men were partners against the women and only said good night when they were ahead a game. Like the bottle of wine, all the gifts from the Bronfmans were dear: tooled leather book covers, linen handkerchiefs edged in lace, hand-woven silk ties and shawls. These luxuries came from Saks, Bloomingdale's, and

later, Bendel's, where Harold worked as a messenger when the
milk company retired him from his route. Sabine saved the
boxes and ribbons. Harold was proud of the fact that he had
delivered the Duchess of Windsor's fur coat to their apartment in the Waldorf-Astoria; the Duke had offered him a cigar
and told him that he, too, was German. When Sabine saw
the Duke waiting on the corner of Lexington Avenue for the
light to change, she smiled at him as if they had a friend in
common.

She was introduced to another Maria, a shipmate younger
and more reticent than her former neighbor, also married to
a man named Harold. Sabine took this as a good omen and
sought them out at mealtimes. One evening, instead of the
usual jello and cookies for dessert, the cook baked a cake with
a sugar bell stuck onto the top layer. After dinner, someone
produced a radio and Maria and her husband danced, often
apart, but only a fingertip's length, and always ending in each
other's arms. They smiled at their admirers, never once looking
down at their feet even as the steps became more intricate. It
seemed to Sabine they must have been dancing this way forever.
When she found out the couple had only recently married, she
avoided their table, not wishing to intrude.

Conversation with the other passengers was difficult; most
grew tired of having to repeat themselves. With each repeti-
tion the sentences became simpler, the adjectives and adverbs
gone the way of subtlety. Sabine was included in the fun, but
only laughed at the broadest humor, those jokes enlivened by
gestures. The Indian women pointed out an eagle or a pod of
whales as if to amuse a child. Sabine fished in her pocketbook
for her glasses.

Mostly she smiled and concentrated on the food: watery

soup and crackers, soft bread with no ends worth chewing on, but once in awhile, hard rolls, salad greens laced with cabbage and carrots for interest, a piece of meat roasted beyond recognition, and lots of potatoes and gravy, which Sabine favored. And there was always a dish of peanuts set out next to the ash trays for the cardplayers.

During the days she addressed postcards. "I started all this traveling too late," she wrote, mostly to old girlfriends from the homeland, touchstones for her reminiscences of Lottie and Hans. Sadly, Gretel had forgotten the trip to East Prussia. She wrote to Gus' sisters, who were surely taking this opportunity to gossip while she was too far away to defend herself. The older she got, the tighter Sabine sealed the envelopes on her letters; tape and wildlife stamps secured the backs. Inside, she spoke of the scenery and fluctuations in temperature.

Sabine left her cabin as often as weather permitted, keeping record of the laps she made around the small deck area reserved for the strolling passengers, calculating the hours until the next meal, counting the Indian children, to ease her mind that none had fallen overboard; where were their mothers when they wandered too close to the railings? She worried that, in her absence, her own grandchildren, at that very moment, had slipped away from their less vigilant parents.

Sitting quietly on the aluminum deck chair was next to impossible, her hands and mind idle; Sabine rose stiffly and took another turn, her steps measured and unsure. She stripped the blanket from her bed and wrapped it around her legs, its military origins reminding her of Rudy. Then, of course, Lottie. The dead claiming her thoughts while she was awake, her dreams when she napped: Hans and her mother. Worst of all, her father, because she hadn't been with him when he died.

In the early hours when the ship had tied up and was taking on freight and most of the passengers slept, two of the construction workers grabbed Sabine firmly under each arm and led her down the gangplank. The streets of Haines, Alaska were icy and they trooped single file--she safely wedged between the two men. In a tavern Sabine sat on a stool drinking beer. She was intrigued by the stuffed polar bear that stood as sentinel outside the restroom door, stroked its nose. That night, Sabine fell into her hard bunk, the first time she had ever gone to bed without brushing her teeth.

On the final evening of the voyage, she dined alone with the captain. Maria and her new husband were honeymooning in the interior of British Columbia; the others had been put off one by one on the drizzly islands to resume their communal isolated lives.

The captain made a toast. "À vôtre santé," he said loudly, mistaking Sabine's accent. He was a nice-looking man; she was surprised she was still susceptible to that. They ate mostly in silence, but she was glad she had saved her best dress for last.

On the drive home, she regaled her grandchildren with her adventures up north. Although she and her friends only walked into Haines and had a few beers there, Sabine said she felt she really knew Alaska. Sensing they were losing interest, she added, "I saw a polar bear." Well, let her daughter look at her like that; it wasn't strictly a lie.

In the absence of any contraband liquor or cigarettes, she was tempted not to declare the few trinkets she had purchased, but then offered up the plush toy seal and wooden totem pole to the customs inspector. The man, noting something in her face, perhaps a look of residual guilt, asked to see her passport. After hesitating a moment, all the resistance she could muster, she handed it over.

Sabine gazed wistfully back at the fields as they sped past, wondering out loud what might have happened had they tried to sneak across the border at an unmarked location.

"Most likely, we would have been shot at by some local farmer," Tessa said. Lottie had smuggled meat under her coat into East Berlin when that city was newly divided by the Wall; Sabine remembered her sister stayed two weeks beyond the date allotted on her visa.

There was another trip, this time by plane to a warmer climate. Sabine preferred the hotel pool to the Caribbean and sat in the shade of a tower in which a pirate once lived. She didn't venture into the hills to eat or dance with the other tourists because the maitre d' of the hotel restaurant advised against it, which was just as well, because the thought of those winding mountain roads and eating the native food made her stomach nervous.

Along the way there were a few injuries, to be expected of a woman of advancing age: a broken kneecap when she fell while clambering on board the freighter, discovered long after the trip was over, a twisted ankle getting off the small connecting plane that brought her to Tessa's house. Sabine wasn't paying attention when the metal step was rolled alongside, still thrilled that the pilot had put her in the navigator's seat during the flight and clamped the earphones on her head.

When it came time for Sabine to fill out the insurance

papers in the emergency room, she asked, "Am I signing my life away?"

Tessa laughed at her mother's exaggerated fears. "Now you're just like them," she said, referring to Charlotte's family; one or another member was always in a cast. Her niece had a broken collarbone from a bicycle accident; Charlotte's husband injured his foot when a log he was chopping rolled onto it. Only her sister seemed immune, remaining robustly intact.

Both daughters were afraid to take their mother in. They had little experience with old people, their grandparents having all died before either one of them was born. Living the closest, Charlotte had to drive Sabine to the doctor when she fell down. She called the West Coast to report the latest injury.

"Mother makes me feel like a fool," she complained. Her sister wondered if they could possibly be talking about the same woman.

Of her stay in Charlotte's house, Sabine said, "I tried to keep out of the way; I don't like to interfere."

But she couldn't coax the children to play board games with her; all of the boxes had pieces missing.

"Did Charlotte think we wouldn't notice? Does she believe we're stupid?"

There was no more talk about travels to exotic places. Instead, discussions never veered far from the essentials: supermarket specials and their accompanying coupons, bills and the phone company's ability to hide its duplicity in so many slips of paper. After a brief stab at liberated widowhood, the old Sabine reappeared. Distilled.

She shuttled from Charlotte's couch to Tessa's sofa, nonstop, between east and west, touching down at home only when some emergency arose: a burst pipe, a tree branch deposited on the roof during a wind storm. Sabine didn't wish to dwell long in the calamitous present.

With each visit, her daughters saw their mother's capacity for physical movement diminish, while that agile childish part of her brain leapt backwards in time to the earliest, most vivid and cherished memories, the middle years entirely skipped over; either uneventful or too painful to relive. A sense of urgency entered Sabine's voice as she retold the stories, the necessity to transmit the details, however sketchy, before they too became diminished. Her leg up in a splint, her arm in a makeshift dishtowel sling, here was the perfect example of what happens when you take chances and leave home. Passing on dire predictions, frightening the timid, her legacy to the next generation.

"If you ever want to get rid of the old photo albums," Tessa said offhandedly one day, "I wouldn't mind having them." Before they were misplaced, or suffered water damage. Irrefutable proof in black and white of the good times. Just to balance things.

DAUGHTER

24

It's cruel of me to flaunt my mobility this way. My mother, constrained by a bad knee, watches as I lace up my running shoes. Before she can say anything--caution against traffic or menacing dogs--I'm outside and down the driveway with an exaggerated burst of speed, running flat out until I'm sure she no longer sees me, then pant up the hill, making good my escape.

I'm defenseless against the old stories, the half truths and theories of family madness exhaustively revisited. It's all she wants to talk about. She's being lured back into the past; I won't join her there.

With each change of season I meticulously and ruthlessly clear out the closets. And there aren't too many items in the attic I would be sorry to part with, but mother keeps sending more useless stuff infused with the smoke of stale cigars, weighing me down, pinning me in one place.

She brought the bugs with her, in the leather suitcases. Or they stowed away under a flap of one of those parcels she's always shipping off. Now they've gotten into everything. It looks as if ashes have been scattered onto the oriental rug; the black medallions are speckled with white tufts where the warp shows through. The bugs are partial to the rare species of moth poorly preserved under the glass of the Brazilian rose-wood tray; they've devoured the dark ovals in the centers of the priceless blue wings. They love the Christmas decorations, feeding on the boiled glue used to repair the treetop angel.

Mother brought in old age, dragging it around the house, shuffling it in front of her slippers. At night I stand outside her door listening to the rattling snores, the ragged intakes of air. Once I monitored my babies' breaths, straining to perceive the rise and fall in the tiny chests, relieved to feel the soft puffs of air against my fingertips. I lift up my mother's eyelids; the pupils are rolled back in her head. I place a penny on each lid to weigh it shut. But in the morning, the hoary presence is at breakfast.

This can't be it. This can't be all. But there is the evidence of my parents' lives and those of the uncles and aunts. No surprises. No grand expectations, that old insurance against disappointment. Some days, the worst days, I make a fist with the fingers clenched so tightly the nails dig into the palm of my hand. Mother would say I'm only hurting myself.

Taking large gulps of air helps. After a reasonable, calming interval during which I lean on a fence and admire the langorous eating habits of a disinterested cow, I reluctantly retrace my steps, the wind at my back.

In the meantime, I'm sure mother hasn't been idle; the demons won't catch her resting. Yesterday, she propped herself in front of the linen closet and rearranged the shelves by color, folding the towels so the fringes weren't visible, stroking the familiar tablecloths. She limped into the garden and packed the rhubarb leaves around the camellia plants, a serviceable, ugly humus, and wiped at the windows with one of Greg's old undershirts. The windows aren't cleaned to her satisfaction. I've never learned Rudy's secret. Whether I use rags, newspaper or chamois or alter the cleaning solution--kerosene, ammonia versus vinegar and water--the outcome is the same.

Even the final buffing of the panes with the flat of my hand won't entirely remove the streaks.

Now mother is in my room, making the bed, attacking the down comforter, her wedding present, redistributing the feathers. Greg says that if we part, the comforter is his to keep. The unsettled question of its custody is why, I tell my mother, we decided not to go through with the divorce.

It was just a sack of feathers with a pretty damask cover when she gave it to us. I had it quilted. Mother wasn't satisfied with the results and is sure she could have done better. This would have been impossible; after sewing, the feathers were blown in. She tells me again about the woman who spent her days sorting, picking off the quills, the discarded feathers floating up into the trees, tingeing the branches with untimely snow. Her task was a useful one in a continuing tradition; it was the job given to old people who had the patience to perform it. In the absence of such work, mother has to make do with fluffing and reshaping.

"Are you sure the people in the factory didn't replace the down with chicken feathers?"

"As sure as I can be of anything," I say and smile. Mother smiles back. She does that a lot now. The tube on her hearing aid has become unglued. She says it's not worth fixing; she can't tell the difference when it's on. I'm the only person, she claims, she can't hear.

Wearing a hearing aid offends her vanity, but her only concession to artifice is a yearly permanent. When she first arrives, I pluck and tweeze and color, these ministrations the only gifts she'll accept. She looks years younger. But we both know she won't keep it up. She rails about the unfairness of it all; my mother alone bears these flaws, inherited defects in face and figure. The truth is she doesn't feel she's worth the effort.

"Now we don't want to put all the blame on your father," she says. For years I believed he was the one who made her feel badly about herself. Actually, he was only exploiting something in her character. It made her stay with him, first out of love, and then out of fear. It took my mother years to realize that the bully in him was as much at fault as the thing it was in her he couldn't love.

She sits at the dining room table, her leg up on a chair. "Such a fuss." She exclaims over the cloth, the candles, the jar of field flowers, not quite sure this is for her benefit.

"I used to make an effort, too, didn't I? When you're younger, you put yourself out."

I reassure her. There were boiled green eggs St. Patrick's Day morning, a lamb cake at Easter. Halloween costumes hand sewn. Much more of that sort of thing than I do for my own children. Than I'm doing for my mother now; each morning and evening I cream the papery soles of her feet.

She's content. Her greatest happiness is when my husband is absent from dinner as he is now, and we eat alone. Dinner is the climax of the day and all general movement should be towards that. When we shop and I don't stop at the grocery store or bakery or defrost anything by six o'clock, mother becomes agitated, moving things around on the kitchen counter, hinting. She thinks I'm putting myself in unnecessary danger waiting until the last moment. When Greg comes home late and the food isn't on the table waiting, she tries to smooth things over, nervously fussing. My intercessor, for years absorbing my father's rages. When I suggest my husband warm up the food himself, she can't bear it.

"It's not my fault," she says, "This is not how I raised my daughter."

She watches me as I eat. "Not so fast," she insists, which has the contrary effect. She recites the ingredients of her favorite recipes but won't be persuaded to cook. She peers at me closely as if I'm an oddity, as if she can't quite believe how I've turned out. So unlike her.

"You always wear brown," mother says, in an effort to define me. Worse, and even more damning, "You never sing around the house."

I do play the piano, but take no delight in the Viennese waltzes she requests; is one supposed to be nostalgic for an earlier, less happy time?

At meals, when I inquire if she wants seconds, I have to repeat the question twice before she relents, fearful there won't be enough for us all.

"Charlotte's a good cook, too," mother says, as if I need convincing. There should be no harsh words between sisters, regardless of how we feel. She wants us to be civil to one another.

"You girls don't fight over my jewelry when I'm gone. Charlotte can have the good dishes," she says, still possessing sufficient treasure to buy my attention. She tells me I'll inherit my grandmother's tea set when I know Charlotte has always coveted it. All I want is the other Majolica vase, almost identical to the one I broke. It's a bit larger, but the same velvety blackness is interrupted by bands of oranges and yellows, suggestive of a sunset. If I had it in my possession, I could go back before I met the young man, when I was convinced of the soundness of my marriage. But Charlotte deserves the vase; I feel I already had one chance and blew it.

I suspect mother would rather live with me than with my sister. But she doesn't know what it's really like around here, doesn't sense the missing pieces. All she knows is that Charlotte's husband ignores his wife when he comes home from work and yells at her in public. Mother sees too much of my father in him. She believes in not raising your voice, having learned the futility of trying to outshout someone unwavering in his convictions. Sentences modulated in even, clipped tones are just as deadly. Or chilling silence. Anything to avoid a confrontation.

After an uneventful courtship and a hasty marriage, mother discovered she had left the keys to all of her suitcases at her brother's house. She made up her mind then that if her new husband so much as raised his voice when she told him, she would walk out the door. It was one of the few times my father kept his mouth shut; after all, the contents in the bags were of little concern to him. He had been married a month and was out of work when he first spoke sharply to his wife. Mother was afraid to talk back, tell him never to do that again; his outbursts were preferable to violence. If he touched her in anger, she believed he might kill her.

Greg, my husband, is quiet. He has little self knowledge, is more frustrated than angry with his life and retreats into his work. We don't fight; we gave that up four years ago. I struck him then because I saw no other way to get his attention, the insulting words no longer hitting their mark. I felt that I had gone as far as I dared go. He pays attention to my mother because he believes her presence is temporary. Besides, she defers to him. When I want my mother to do something for her own good, I ask Greg to suggest it. When he's kind to her, I can forgive him anything. We wait until we get into bed before talking things out. A plasterboard wall is all that stands between my mother and the secrets of my married life.

"Not so loud," I whisper.

"You know Sabine is deaf."

"She hears what she wants to."

I think she must be afraid, all this falling down, afraid where she'll end up. I want to be reassuring, but can't promise I'll never put her someplace else. Charlotte and I want what is in her best interest. We're not it. We're all she has.

And there's no comfort to be gained from reviewing our past history. When it was just the two of us at our summer home, more often than not I left my mother alone, taking off for the beach early in the day. She declined my invitations. The sand was too hot. There was no shade. The water was not to be trusted.

"When your father and I were first married, going to the beach was a pleasure. Then, at least, you could swim and not worry about what you were going to bump into."

While I was toasting myself, slathered in a baby-oil and iodine concoction, mother, wearing a visor and long-sleeved blouse, picked strawberries at the farm down the road, then, ladling in too much sugar, turned them into a year's worth of thick jam. She fussed at things then too, pruning bushes with an aggressive hand, making me swear not to tell my father. Using an old scythe, she attacked the weeds and fashioned a lawn of sorts, taming what her husband had allowed to revert to nature. I wondered at her energy while the sun made me lethargic and, after lunch, I laid down on the cot under a tree. She didn't want too much, just that I dry a few dishes, not get into trouble, remain a child for as long as possible. Which is why, when my mother visits, I can't ride my bicycle, or fly my child's kite; I won't conspire in her image of me as an adult who's never grown up.

My father had bigger plans. At a safe remove, and under his stern direction, Charlotte and I, along with our male cousins, pulled on the ropes until every last tree on the property tagged with an orange ribbon had been felled. Two streets away, teenage girls were constructing a garage for their family; my father drove by slowly so we all could admire the workmanship. Later, he would point out the cinder block wall of our own garage which his daughters cemented and where the first, premature cracks appeared.

On the way to the airport, I stop the car to watch an eagle fishing the river. "Take out your glasses, mom," I say, but know she's saving them for later when she'll need them more. "You're missing too much."

She counters, "You're just like me. You find joy in small things."

I wish I could disagree. I, too, pick strawberries in the summers, even though we can't eat them fast enough.

The camellia blossoms are lying on the seat between us, in a plastic bag. At first mother took these back with her to show my father. Now it's his sisters, my aunts, whose grudging admiration she extracts for the oversized blooms; here is something of which her daughter is capable, something that matters.

As we approach the airport, we realize time is short. What

reticence we feel disappears; we're tired of sparring and wish to get in a few good blows before departure. In the midst of an account of old wrongs perpetrated by my father on us both, mother says quietly, "You know, the one thing he never forgave you for was raising your voice to him; you didn't show him the proper respect." I suspect she shares this complaint. Unlike my mother, I refused to fear him. My father never had to listen to the recital of grievances I've just endured; she waited until he was dead to utter them. I remember rushing from the dining room table when speech failed me, banging the bedroom door as my final statement. I recall the spare eulogy at my father's funeral and think he had the last word, after all.

I held myself in check then, the anger tempered by residual affection. I find the same anger rising in me now. I want to shake my mother, "You have misjudged me again, know nothing about what I care for." She revealed past confidences of mine to my father. "You would twist my words and willfully misunderstand; I can't trust you enough not to do that." But to openly declare our estrangement would be hurtful; it is bad enough it exists between sisters.

I say nothing. Instead, I am falsely contrite. I blame my behavior on my youthful temper. "I couldn't sit by and listen to him any longer. I was a teenager then." This, my mother can understand. After all, I was his child, too.

She won't rest until I exonerate him for not having loved me. It seems I can't. It should be enough that I loved him in spite of his failure.

"Someday, you'll be sorry," she says, confusing our stories. "I left my father, too. My mother was dead, he was alone; I'll never forgive myself."

"Children are supposed to leave their parents," I respond,

her frequent presence in my house giving this the lie.

They allow me to accompany her onto the plane. "Don't take my arm; I'll take yours," she insists. It's a subtle distinction in her mind.

I point out the wheelchair at the gate and reassure her there will be one waiting at the other end of the flight.

"Am I really that old?" she asks. "It would be nice to be sixty again; sixty is a nice age."

I tell her that wheelchairs are for people with broken kneecaps and buckle her into her seat.

"No more basement stairs for awhile." I imagine my mother going down to retrieve a jar of strawberry jam from the root cellar, putting her foot on the first tread. Perhaps she's left the gas stove on all this time. When she flicks the light switch, whoosh, up she'll go, like one of those cartoon characters. It won't be as simple as that. It won't be as sudden.

The plane is late. I don't dare leave until it takes off. I can look into the cockpit and see the pilot tapping on the instruments; perhaps the waiting is getting to him, too. At any moment, the steps will unfurl and they'll send her back to me. Finally, the plane begins to move. I wave at the row of anonymous windows. Already mother will have adjusted her headset to its maximum volume, tuning in the pilot's voice, believing his calm, measured intonation, and her own attentiveness, will keep them safely aloft.

"Damn it, old woman, why didn't you tell me how sick he was."

The question will keep coming up. Just when I've had time to recover and resume singing around the house, she'll visit again. She'll have no trouble finding me here, hobbled by the past, trying to extricate myself from under a bug-infested box of photographs or brittle sheet music newly arrived in the mail. Home will never be far enough.

Getting into the car, I notice the forgotten camellias, sat upon, crushed in their plastic. White scabs cling to the undersides of the mottled leaves. Less than perfect. Just as well, I think; there really is no one left to impress. And the revenge, such as it is, so slight.

REFERENCE

Frazer, H. T., and J. O'Sullivan. Fall, 1978. *"Forgotten Women of World War II: Wives of Conscientious Objectors in Civilian Public Service."* PEACE & CHANGE, Vol. V, Nos. 2 & 3.

A NOTE ABOUT THE AUTHOR

Norma Shainin was born in New York City and now resides with her husband in rural Western Washington State. She has always loved books and worked for a publisher, bookseller and print shop before becoming a writer. Although she considers herself a novelist, early on, one of her short stories was chosen for the PEN Syndicated Fiction Project and, more recently, another story was included in New Millennium Writings.

A NOTE ON THE TYPE

Centaur MT, the font used in this book, was designed by Bruce Rogers, who was renowned for his artistry in combining type and ornament. His inspiration was Nicholas Jenson's printing in 1470 of a work by Eusebius. The uppercase letters, set by hand, were first used by the Metropolitan Museum of Art in 1914; the complete font was cast in 1915 in 14 point. (The name was derived from the handset printing in 1915 by Mrs. Rogers of Maurice de Guérin's book, The Centaur.) Rogers later made a version for Monotype's typesetting machines and, by 1929, several other sizes were being used. Originally, Centaur was roman only, but at Rogers' request, Monotype added an italic based on drawings by Frederic Warde, which in turn were an interpretation of the work of sixteenth-century printer Ludovico degli Arrighi. Elegant in its proportions, Centaur is a testament to Bruce Rogers' skill in transitioning from handwork to machine.

Printed and bound by
Thomson-Shore
Michigan

Designed by Jennifer Shainin